Gill Books
Hume Avenue, Park West, Dublin 12

www.gillbooks.ie

Gill Books is an imprint of M.H. Gill & Co.

Text © GAA Museum 2016
Photography © www.sportsfile.com /
GAA Museum 2016
Design/format copyright © Teapot Press Ltd. 2016

ISBN: 978-0-7171-7071-5

This book was created and produced by Teapot Press Ltd.

Written by Mark Reynolds, Niamh McCoy,
Julianne McKeigue & Joanne Clarke
Photography supplied by www.sportsfile.com and the GAA Museum,
www.crokeparke.ie/gaamuseum

Designed by Alyssa Peacock & Tony Potter
Edited by Elizabeth Golding, Fiona Biggs & Ruth Mahony

Printed in Europe

This book is typeset in Dax, Minion and Albertus.

A CIP catalogue record for this book is available
from the British Library.

5 4 3 2 1

THE
POCKET BOOK
OF THE
GAA

MARK REYNOLDS, NIAMH McCOY
JULIANNE McKEIGUE & JOANNE CLARKE

Gill Books

Contents

About the GAA

The Gaelic Athletic Association (GAA), or Cumann Lúthchleas Gael in the Irish language, is a 32-county of Ireland sporting and cultural organisation that also has a presence on all five continents.

The GAA is Ireland's largest sporting organisation, promoting Gaelic games and culture and lifelong participation in the organisation.

The main GAA sports are Gaelic football, hurling, handball and rounders and the Association also works with its sister organisations to promote the games of camogie (the women's version of hurling) and ladies Gaelic football.

At the core of the GAA is an amateur ethos. The Association is community-based and volunteer-led, relying on volunteers in every community across Ireland to run their games and competitions. Players in all codes are amateurs, and although the training, commitment and skills necessary to play the sports are on a par with those required of professional sports people, GAA players do not get paid. They play for a love of Gaelic games and the honour of representing their local community at both club and county level.

The GAA has over one million members, with more than 2,300 GAA clubs located in Ireland and across the globe. The best players from these clubs are selected to play for their county teams and these teams compete in inter-county competitions, including national leagues and the All-Ireland championships. The Association has its headquarters at Croke Park on the north side of Dublin city. This modern stadium is the largest in Ireland, and one of the largest in Europe, with the capacity to hold 82,300 spectators.

The All-Ireland finals take place at Croke Park every September between the two qualifying counties. Teams secure their place in the final after competing successfully in a championship-structured series of games, which begins in their province (Ulster, Munster, Leinster or Connacht). Traditionally the hurling finals take place on the first Sunday of the month, the camogie finals on the second Sunday, the Gaelic football finals on the third Sunday and the ladies football finals on the fourth Sunday of the month. These finals

MONAGHAN line up behind the Anglo-Celt cup at the Ulster senior football final, Donegal v Monaghan, St Tiernach's Park, Clones, County Monaghan, 19 July 2015.

are some of the most high-profile events on the Irish sporting calendar.

Underpinning the Association is a democratic structure that sees voluntary members at various levels elect officers to serve on positions on a variety of tiers up to and including the position of Uachtarán (President). This democratic process extends to the committees who organise the games at local club level, as well as at county, provincial and national levels. All administrators, regardless of rank or level of involvement, are members of one of the Association's clubs.

Along with other national sports bodies, the GAA is a member of the Irish Sports Council. The Council works in partnership with these national governing bodies (NGBs) to develop their sports in the areas of planning, administration, IT, coaching, equipment, ethics and anti-doping.

Gaelic Football and Hurling

Gaelic football is a field game that has developed as a distinct but somewhat similar game to Australian Rules football.

DAVID MORAN (KERRY) AND PAUL FLYNN (DUBLIN) in action during the 2015 All-Ireland senior football final.

The ball used in Gaelic football is round, slightly smaller than a soccer ball. It can be carried in the hand for a distance of four steps and can be kicked or 'hand-passed', a striking motion using the hand or fist. After every four steps, the ball must be either bounced or 'soloed', an action of dropping the ball onto the foot and kicking it back into the hand. You may not bounce the ball twice in a row. To score, you put the ball over the crossbar by foot or hand/fist for one point, or under the crossbar and into the net by foot (or hand/fist in certain circumstances) for a goal, the latter being the equivalent of three points.

Hurling is believed to be the world's oldest field game. The stick, or hurley (camán in Irish), is curved outwards at the end to provide the striking surface. The ball (sliotar) is similar in size to a hockey ball but has raised ridges. You may strike the ball on the ground or in the air. Unlike hockey, you may pick the ball up with your hurley and carry it

POSTER

from 1881, showing the various skills of hurling.

CONOR WHELAN
(Galway) competes
with Kilkenny's
Kieran Joyce and
Cillian Buckley
during the 2015
All-Ireland senior
hurling final.

for not more than four steps in the hand. After those steps, you may bounce the ball on the hurley and back to the hand, but you are forbidden to catch the ball more than twice. To get around this, one of the skills is running with the ball balanced on the hurley. To score, you put the ball over the crossbar with the hurley or with your foot for one point, or under the crossbar and into the net with the hurley or with your foot for a goal, the latter being the equivalent

of three points.

Both hurling and Gaelic football are played on a pitch up to 145 metres long and 90 metres wide. The goalposts are similar to those used in rugby, with the crossbar lower than in rugby and slightly higher than in soccer. Gaelic football and hurling teams are made up of 15 players.

Officials for both sports comprise a referee and two linesmen – linesmen indicate when the ball leaves the field of play at the side and mark 45 (football) and 65 (hurling) frees. A 45 is when the ball is played across the endline and outside the goalposts by the defending team – the opposing team is awarded a free kick off the ground from the 45-metre line. A 65 is the same as a 45, but the free puck is from the 65-metre line. There are also four umpires to assist the referee in controlling the games and to assist the linesmen in positioning frees. The umpires signal a goal by raising a green flag, placed to the left of the goal. A point is signalled by raising a white flag, placed to the right of goal. A 45 and a 65 are signalled by the umpire raising his or her outside arm.

Women and the GAA

When the GAA was formed in 1884, women did not have a place in the Association, apart from on the sidelines as spectators cheering on the men.

LAOIS PLAYERS
celebrate after
winning the All-
Ireland junior camogie
championship final.

Since these early days, the role of women in Gaelic games has changed dramatically. In 1903 a ladies hurling team known as Keatings was set up in

Dublin by Máire Ní Chinnéide, and in 1904 a second Dublin club, Cú Chulainn's, emerged. The formation of these two clubs led to the first recorded public game of camogie in July 1904 when the sides met at the Meath Agricultural Society Grounds. The Camogie Association (Cumann Camógaíochta na nGael) was then founded, with Máire Ní Chinnéide as the first president. The aim of the Camogie Association was to provide women in Ireland with their own version of hurling. At the time, women could not wear short skirts, shorts or trousers, so they had to play in restrictive clothing comprising a blouse and long heavy skirt covering the ankles. A special rule had to be drawn up for camogie, stating that players could not use their long dresses to stop the sliotar! Throughout the years, the sport of camogie has developed and grown in popularity.

Ladies football is one of the fastest-growing female sports in Europe. The Ladies Gaelic Football Association (LGFA) was founded in 1974 and the sport was established quickly at this time in eight counties – Laois, Offaly, Tipperary, Galway, Kerry, Cork, Roscommon and Waterford. This strong foundation and interest in the sport meant that the games spread rapidly and there are now over 1,000 clubs in Ireland and overseas. Ladies football teams compete annually for the Brendan Martin Cup, which was first awarded to Tipperary in 1974 after they beat Offaly in the All-Ireland final. With live television coverage contributing to an increase in popularity of ladies football, it's no wonder that the finals of 2015 were the highest-attended women's sporting event of that year, with a crowd of 31,083 spectators looking on in Croke Park.

SUPPORTERS
at the 2015
All-Ireland ladies
football final.

Camogie

Camogie is a sport played by 100,000 women in Ireland and abroad.

The sport is administered by the Camogie Association (An Cumann Camógaíochta).

The structure of the Camogie Association is similar to that of the GAA – its Annual Congress takes place every spring to decide on policy and major changes, while its Executive Committee (Ard Chomhairle) deals with short-term issues and governance. There are four provincial councils, while the county boards are responsible for managing their own affairs.

SERIES OF IMAGES
entitled 'Ladies Hurling Match at Nenagh', as published in the *Weekly Examiner* in 1924.

Competitions are run at club, county, provincial and international levels, in addition to schools and inter-collegiate competitions. The two main competitions that take place are the inter-county senior national league, which is staged during the winter–spring months, with four divisions of teams graded by ability. In the summer months, counties compete for the All-Ireland senior camogie title, with the final played in Croke Park in September and the winners awarded the O'Duffy Cup.

The game itself is almost identical to hurling except for the following differences:

- Goalkeepers wear the same colours as outfield players. This is because no special rules apply to the goalkeeper and so there is no need for officials to differentiate between goalkeeper and outfielders.
- A camogie player can hand-pass a score (forbidden in hurling since 1980).
- Camogie games last 60 minutes, two 30-minute halves (senior inter-county hurling games last 70 minutes, two 35-minute halves). Ties are resolved by multiple 2×10-minute sudden death extra time periods; in these, the first team to score wins.
- Dropping the camogie stick to hand-pass the ball is permitted.

- A smaller sliotar – commonly known as a size 4 sliotar – is used in camogie, whereas hurlers play with a size 5 sliotar.
- If a defending player hits the sliotar wide, a 45-metre puck, rather than a 65, is awarded to the opposition.
- After a score, the goalkeeper pucks out from the 13-metre line instead of the endline, as in hurling.
- The metal band on the camogie stick must be covered with tape.
- Side-to-side charges are forbidden.
- Two points are awarded for a score direct from a sideline cut.

CORK CAPTAIN
Ashling Thompson lifts the O'Duffy Cup in 2015.

Ladies Gaelic Football

Ladies Gaelic football is a team sport for women, very similar to Gaelic football, but administered by a separate organisation – the Ladies Gaelic Football Association (LGFA).

The structure of the LGFA is similar to that of the GAA – its Annual Congress takes place every spring to decide on policy and major changes, while

CORA STAUNTON (Mayo) in action against Aisling Leonard (Kerry) at the Gaelic Grounds, Limerick.

its Executive Committee (Ard Chomhairle) deals with short-term issues and governance. There are four provincial councils, while the county boards are responsible for managing their own affairs.

Competitions are run at club, county, provincial and international levels, in addition to schools and inter-collegiate competitions. There are two main competitions: the inter-county senior national league, which is staged during the winter–spring months, and, in the summer months, the All-Ireland senior ladies football title, with the final played in Croke Park in September and the winners awarded the Brendan Martin Cup.

The game itself is almost identical to Gaelic football except for the following differences:

- A player may pick the ball up directly from the ground, as long as she is standing.
- Most matches last 60 minutes; in the men's game, senior inter-county games last 70 minutes.
- Kickouts may be taken from the hand.
- A countdown clock with a siren is used if available; in the men's game, the referee decides the end of the game.
- It is permitted to change the ball from one hand to the other.

DUBLIN CAPTAIN
Lyndsey Davey leads her team out on to the pitch past the Brendan Martin Cup.

- All deliberate bodily contact is forbidden except when 'shadowing' an opponent, competing to catch the ball or blocking the delivery of the ball.
- A smaller size 4 Gaelic ball is used, compared to the size 5 ball used in the men's game.

GAA Handball

The sport of handball is an important member of the GAA family and was included in the original charter of the Association.

Today GAA handball has its own governing body, including an overall president and four provincial presidents. The aim of this body is to preserve and promote the national game of handball.

PAUL BRADY
(Cavan) in action.
GAA Handball 40 x
20 All-Ireland senior
singles final.

In Ireland there are four separate handball codes, including Four Wall, One Wall, 60 x 30 and Hardball. Singles and doubles championships are held in all four codes. The fast-paced games test many attributes, including speed, endurance and co-ordination.

Four Wall (40 x 20)

- Currently the most popular version of handball in Ireland.
- Played indoors in an enclosed space with a roof and four walls (similar to a squash court).
- This version of handball is played internationally across 10 countries.

One Wall (Wallball)

- As the name suggests, this form of the sport needs just one wall and a ball and is the fastest growing handball code.
- Played both indoors and outdoors.

60 x 30 (Softball)

- This game is regarded as the traditional Irish handball code and is played in a bigger alley.
- Traditionally played in the summer months as the courts were outdoors originally, but new purpose-built indoor courts are now also in use.

Hardball

- Hardball is the most ancient form of handball. It is also the fastest of the four codes.

Handball Alleys

A common sight in many Irish towns and villages
are the stone handball alleys (known as 'big alleys'),
which were built on communal grounds such as fair
greens. These alleys played a vital role in community
life, providing entertainment as well as a place for
locals to gather. Many still remain that date back to
the late 19th century.

HANDBALL ALLEY,
Oldcastle, Meath.

Handball on an International Stage

As well as being played in Ireland, handball is popular in North America, Australia, the UK, Spain and Puerto Rico, and is now spreading to countries such as the Netherlands, Argentina, Japan, India, Italy and Belgium.

Handball Star Michael 'Ducksy' Walsh

Michael 'Ducksy' Walsh from Kilkenny won a record 38 All-Ireland senior titles between 1985 and 2001. He secured a remarkable 13-in-a-row and 16 titles within 17 years in the singles grade, a feat that is unlikely to be equalled.

HANDBALL STAR MICHAEL 'DUCKSY' WALSH

in attendance at the launch of the 2012 World Handball Championships.

Poc Fada

Poc Fada is the Irish language term for Long Puck and refers to an annual All-Ireland competition which tests the skills of top hurlers.

THREE BOYS standing at the start of the Poc Fada circuit in the Cooley Mountains, Louth, 1961.

The senior Poc Fada finals are usually held in July in the Cooley Mountains in County Louth on a course that measures just over five kilometres. The Setanta Cup is awarded to the player who takes the lowest number of pucks with a hurley to move the sliotar around the course. Ties are broken based on the distance of the player's last puck. A pairs' competition (Comórtas Beirte), in which players are randomly assigned partners, is also part of the tournament.

BRENDAN CUMMINS
(Tipperary) competing
in the 2014 Poc Fada
competition.

The Poc Fada tournament was founded in 1960 by Fr Pól Mac Sheáin, and the first All-Ireland competition took place in 1961. The concept of Poc Fada originates in Irish legend when, as a boy called Setanta, the warrior Cúchulainn set out from his home, hitting the sliotar in front of him and running ahead to catch it.

Throughout the years, many hurling stars have taken part in Poc Fada, most notably legendary Tipperary hurling goalkeeper Brendan Cummins, who had won the event nine times by 2015. Other Poc Fada legends include Ger Cunningham of Cork and Michael Shaughnessy of Galway.

GAA Rounders

GAA Rounders is the fourth official sport of the GAA.

Along with Gaelic football, hurling and handball, rounders was included in the original GAA charter in 1884.

The sport is a bat and ball game with limited contact, not dissimilar to baseball. The ball used in rounders is a sliotar. It is generally agreed that baseball has its roots in the sport of rounders. It is believed that early Irish emigrants brought the game to the US.

Rounders is played by all age groups and is particularly popular in primary schools where it develops hand–eye co-ordination.

The sport includes mixed teams, where males and females play together, and it is played both competitively and recreationally.

Rules of the Game

Rounders is played by two opposing teams (fielding and batting). The pitcher stands facing home base and throws the ball underarm to the batter. The batter must strike the sliotar into the field of play and then run to first base, while the fielding team try to gain possession of the ball and throw it to a base–minder. There are 25 metres between each base

and a total of 100 metres for a home run.

The aim is for the batting side to score as many runs as they can before the fielding team put three players out. A run is when a batter strikes the ball and has proceeded through all three bases before touching home base. A batter is considered 'out' for a number of reasons:

- They fail to strike a good ball after three attempts.
- They strike the last good ball into 'foul ground'.
- They strike a good ball, but it is caught by a fielder.
- The base is tagged (by a member of the fielding team) before the batter arrives at the base.

Scór

The GAA is more than a sporting organisation. It includes the Scór competition, which is at the heart of many GAA clubs and is the social element of the Gaelic Athletic Association, focusing on the Irish traditions of song, dance, music, drama and storytelling.

The competition is structured in a similar way to the GAA All-Ireland hurling and football championships, with competitors taking part in their county contest before moving to the provincial level and, finally,

THE GLENCAR/ MANORHAMILTON team, winners of the 2015 Connacht Scór figure dancing competition.

the All-Ireland final. There is both an adult (Scór Sinsear) and young people's (Scór na nÓg) section, with those under the age of 17 taking part in Scór na nÓg.

GAA club members can take part in eight different events as part of Scór. They are:

- Solo Singing
- Instrumental Music
- Recitation/Story-telling
- Figure Dancing
- Stage Presentation
- Ballad Group
- Set Dancing
- Table Quiz

Scór was established in 1969 to promote Irish cultural activities within the GAA and it traditionally gave members the chance to have fun and meet up with their GAA friends throughout the winter months when there were no Gaelic football or hurling matches.

THE CLARA OFFALY TEAM
during the ballad competition, Scór championship finals, April 2015.

The GAA Structures: Club, County and Province

The GAA Club and Community

The GAA club is the heart of Irish life. The local club has been the bedrock of the GAA since the foundation of the Association in 1884. It is a volunteer-led organisation that involves all members of the community. Playing and non-playing members commit their time, energy and talents on a voluntary basis in the service of the games and their locality.

The club is the focal point of the community – it brings people together in their shared love of the games. Many clubs are the social hub of the town or village and play an important role in bringing communities together.

THE COROFIN TEAM celebrate their victory in the 2015 All-Ireland club championship senior football final.

Today there are over 2,300 GAA clubs in Ireland and throughout the world. They compete within their own county competitions, and at inter-county league and championship level.

Since 1971 the GAA All-Ireland club championships have celebrated the grass-roots level of the Association. The winners of the county championship competitions go on to compete in the provincial club championship at junior, intermediate and senior levels. The winning club within the county goes on to represent their county in the All-Ireland club championship.

The final of this competition is held on St Patrick's Day in Croke Park.

County Board and Inter-county Competitions

Each county is represented by a board that oversees all GAA activity within the county. It manages fixtures within the county and organises the county teams.

In addition to the 32 counties in Ireland, there are also seven overseas county boards: Asia, North America, Australia, Canada, Europe, New York and London.

The best club players within each county are selected to play

THE LONGFORD county football squad.

for their county team. It is a source of pride for them that they are chosen to represent their local community on the county team. The main GAA competitions which involve county teams are the national leagues and the All-Ireland championship.

The national leagues are played in the spring. There are four divisions and teams are promoted and demoted each year. The matches are played almost every weekend until the end of March.

FOOTBALLERS
launching the 2015 Leinster football championship.

The GAA All-Ireland hurling and football championships are played throughout the summer months. Initially teams enter the provincial championships within their own province – Connacht, Leinster, Munster and Ulster. The winners in each sport progress to the All-Ireland series with the ambition of winning the two most prestigious cups in the GAA – the Liam MacCarthy for hurling and the Sam Maguire for football.

Provinces in the GAA

The four provinces of Ireland each have their own provincial council. Britain is also a province in the GAA and has its own council. The counties within each province elect members to represent them on the provincial council. The provincial councils have their own competitions, at club and county level. The inter-county provincial championships have the highest profile and involve local rivalry between neighbouring counties within the province.

The provincial councils also play an important role in the allocation of central funds to the counties and clubs within each province.

GAA Annual Congress

The GAA holds an annual general meeting, Congress, hosted in a different location each year. The previous year is reviewed and proposals on policy or rule changes are debated and voted on by delegates representing all counties.

THE 2014 ANNUAL CONGRESS
in progress in Croke Park.

Other GAA Competitions

- Interprovincial championships: Inter-county players are selected to represent their province in hurling and football
- Football U21 All-Ireland championship: Inter-county under-21 football competition
- Hurling U21 All-Ireland championship – B and C: Inter-county under-21 competition
- Minor championship: Inter-county minor football and hurling competition
- Christy Ring/Nickey Rackard/Lory Meagher: Second-, third- and fourth-tier inter-county championship competitions
- Fitzgibbon Cup: Third-level hurling championship
- Sigerson Cup: Third-level football championship
- Hurling/Shinty: National selection of inter-county hurlers to represent Ireland in a compromise rules game against Scotland
- International Rules series: Compromise rules football with Australia

The Hurley

The stick used in the game of hurling is known as the hurley or hurl, as well as by its Irish language name of camán.

Traditionally the hurley is made from the wood of the ash tree.

The hurley is referred to in Irish literature as early as the 9th century in the story of the mythical figure of Setanta. At that time copper, bronze and even gold were used to band the hurley, depending on the wealth or social standing of the hurler.

A GENERAL VIEW of the modern hurley.

In the past, a local carpenter would help the hurler with the heavier work of cutting the rough shape of the hurley from the tree and then the hurler would shape and smooth the stick. The ash trees were cut down in early winter.

As the game of hurling changed, so too did the hurley itself. It was made lighter and the bás, or boss (the head or opposite end to the stick), was shortened. It was also made slimmer to enable the players to lift the ball. These changes have resulted in a faster and more skilful game.

When choosing a new hurley, it's important to get the correct size for each hurler. A rough guide is that the top of the hurley should reach the player's hip when placed parallel to the leg with the bottom of the hurley on the ground.

TIPPERARY GOALKEEPER
Darren Gleeson's hurleys during a 2015 national hurling league game.

History of the Hurling Helmet

Mícheál Murphy played hurling with University College Cork (UCC) and Blackrock, Cork, from 1960 to 1973. In 1964, while playing a championship match, Mícheál suffered a serious head injury which led him to wear and promote protective headgear for hurling.

HURLING HELMETS.

In October 1966, Mícheál lined out for UCC in the Cork senior hurling final wearing the college's black and red jersey and a motorcycle helmet. This was the first major step in pioneering the idea of protective headgear for hurlers. In 1967, Mícheál imported a Spalding American football helmet and he wore it playing in the Fitzgibbon Cup.

From 1 January 2010, it became compulsory for hurlers at all levels to wear helmets with faceguards while on the field of play.

JOE CANNING
of Galway wearing a
modern hurling helmet.

The Sliotar

The sliotar is the leather ball used in hurling.

In the modern game, the ball is approximately seven centimetres in diameter and weighs about 110–120 grams. The game of hurling dates back over two thousand years and is thought to be one of the oldest sports in the world. Intact sliotars dating back to the 12th century have been discovered in Ireland, preserved in bogs. The balls are made of matted cow's hair, which corresponds with many references in Irish folklore to using cows'-hair balls, both for hurling and as children's playthings.

In 2008 and 2010 the National Museum of Ireland dated a collection of 14 balls that had been discovered in Limerick, Kerry, Clare, Tipperary, Sligo and Mayo. Radio-carbon-dating of samples from the fibres of these balls showed the earliest date range was 1157 to 1227. The oldest sliotar ever discovered was found in Tooraree in County Limerick. The dating of the

SLIOTAR.

National Museum's collection of cow's-hair hurling balls provides evidence of a tradition of making sliotars from cows' hair, which continued in Ireland for more than 500 years.

The design and style of the hair hurling balls did not change until the development of the cork-filled leather sliotar. This is the standardised version of the ball that was used when the GAA was founded in 1884. Modern sliotars have taken things further and have a synthetic core wrapped in leather, rather than a cork filling.

HURLEY AND SLIOTAR.

Hawkeye

One of the most exciting developments at Croke Park in recent years has been the introduction of a new technology known as 'Hawkeye'.

Introduced on Saturday 1 June 2013, the score detection system provides real-time imagery on the stadium's big screen of a ball's trajectory over the posts. This removes any ambiguity over whether a point was scored or missed and assists the referee's decision. The system is used in Croke Park for both hurling and Gaelic football.

Rory Hickey from Clare created history when he became the first referee to use Hawkeye in the 46th minute of a Leinster championship football match between Kildare and Offaly on 1 June 2013. He used the technology to check a 46th-minute shot from Offaly's Peter Cunningham, which turned out to have gone just wide. In a very appropriate

HAWKEYE
is used on the big
screen in Croke Park
during the 2015
All-Ireland minor
hurling final.

partnership agreement, the Specsavers
chain of opticians was announced as the
official sponsor of Hawkeye.

All-Ireland Finals

Held in September in Croke Park, the All-Ireland finals are the culmination of the championships in hurling, football, camogie and ladies Gaelic football, and are among the biggest sporting occasions in Ireland each year.

It is every player's dream to reach an All-Ireland final and to be in with a chance to win a coveted All-Ireland medal. For players, it is the pinnacle of their career.

The finals are sold-out events with 82,300 people in attendance. The rush for tickets begins as soon as each team wins their semi-final – tickets are notoriously difficult to source and do not go on general sale. Instead, members of GAA clubs in the county of

CLARE PLAYERS
prepare for an Anthony Nash penalty, 2013 All-Ireland senior hurling final replay, Clare v Cork.

DONEGAL CELEBRATE
with the Sam Maguire
2012 All-Ireland senior
football final, Donegal
v Mayo.

each competing finalist apply for tickets through the club. The majority of All-Ireland final tickets are allocated to the competing counties. The day is full of colourful pageantry. The Artane Band entertains the crowd, the iconic trophies – the Sam Maguire (football), Liam MacCarthy (hurling), O'Duffy Cup (camogie) and Brendan Martin Cup (ladies football) are on display in the Hogan Stand, awaiting the captains of the winning teams.

The president of Ireland attends the finals and meets the players before the games throw in. There are other dignitaries, VIPs and famous faces in the crowds.

After the final whistle, the winners are presented with the trophy by the president of the GAA, and they do a lap of the pitch to show off the silverware to their celebrating supporters.

The finals attract a global TV audience and are among the most watched TV programmes in Ireland.

The Sam Maguire Cup

The Sam Maguire Cup was presented to the GAA in 1928 as the trophy for the All-Ireland senior football championship.

THE SAM
MAGUIRE CUP.

The original Sam Maguire Cup was first won by Kildare, with William 'Bill' Gannon the first captain to lift the famous cup. In 1987, Mick Lyons became the last ever captain to raise the original cup, when Meath won the All-Ireland final. The original Sam Maguire Cup was retired in 1987, and is now housed in the GAA Museum, with a replica cup being presented to the winners ever since.

The cup, which is modelled on the Ardagh Chalice, was made by Hopkins and Hopkins of

Dublin for £300. The cup was commissioned to commemorate Sam Maguire – a man who had given a lifetime of service to the GAA.

Sam Maguire was born in Dunmanway, County Cork. On leaving school, he joined the Civil Service and was assigned to duty in London. There he grew to prominence – first in the GAA and later in the

THE 1903 LONDON GAELIC FOOTBALL TEAM
Sam Maguire is seated, holding the football.

Irish Republican Brotherhood (IRB). He was an outstanding footballer and played in three All-Ireland finals, in 1900, 1901 and 1903, captaining the London (Hibernians) team on the two latter occasions. As his playing career came to a close, Sam devoted his energy to the legislative side of the Association's affairs. He became a regular delegate to Annual Congress, chairman of the London County Board and, finally, a trustee of Croke Park.

Maguire also played a pivotal role in the Irish War of Independence; it was he who recruited Michael Collins into the republican movement in 1909. Maguire himself reached the rank of Major General and Chief Intelligence Officer of the Irish Republican Army in Britain – during the War of Independence, all major republican operations in Britain were largely under the control of Maguire.

Maguire returned to Ireland in 1923 and took a job with the Irish Civil Service, but on 29 December 1924 he was summarily dismissed without pay from his post, having being accused of conspiring against the government and state services.

Maguire returned to his native Cork. He had been suffering from tuberculosis for some time, and he passed away on 6 February 1927, at the age of 48.

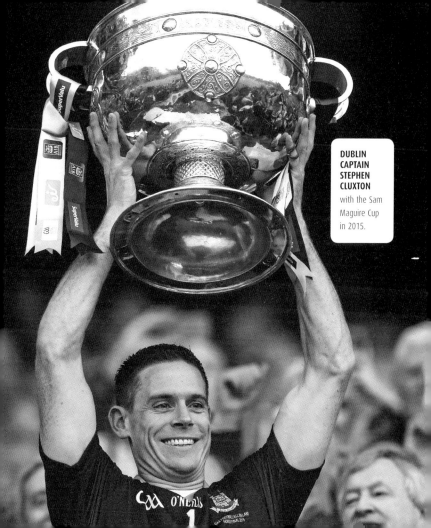

DUBLIN CAPTAIN STEPHEN CLUXTON with the Sam Maguire Cup in 2015.

The Liam MacCarthy Cup

The Liam MacCarthy Cup was presented to the GAA in 1922 as the trophy for the All-Ireland senior hurling championship.

The original Liam MacCarthy Cup was first won by Limerick in 1923 (in what was actually the 1921 final), with Bob McConkey the first captain to lift the famous cup. In 1991, Declan Carr became the last ever captain to raise the original cup, when Tipperary won the All-Ireland final. The original Liam MacCarthy Cup was retired in 1992, and is now housed in the GAA Museum, with a replica cup being presented to the winners ever since.

The cup, which is modelled on an ancient drinking vessel known as a mether, was made by Edmund Johnson Jewellers in Grafton Street, Dublin, and cost £50.

Liam MacCarthy was born in London in 1853 to Irish parents who had left Ireland two

THE LIAM MACCARTHY CUP.

years previously. He grew up in a close-knit Irish community in Peckham, in a home where Irish was the first language. From a young age MacCarthy developed a keen interest in Irish sports, hurling in particular, and was often seen with his hurley on Clapham Common.

In 1875, MacCarthy married Alice Padbury and went to work in her father's cardboard box business. Within a short space of time, MacCarthy established his own cardboard box business, which proved a considerable success. He became heavily involved in GAA circles in London – first as the county board's treasurer, and later as its chairman. He was also vice-president of the Gaelic League and openly supported the Irish nationalist cause at the time when it was not safe to do so in England.

LIAM MACCARTHY.

In 1922 MacCarthy approached the GAA and offered to design and purchase a trophy for the winners of the All-Ireland senior hurling championship – an offer the GAA gladly accepted.

INTERPROVINCIAL FOOTBALL CHAMPIONSHIP 2014.
Michael Darragh MacAuley (Leinster) and Seán Cavanagh (Ulster).

The Railway Cup/ Interprovincial Championships

In the Railway Cup, the best players for from each province in hurling and football are selected to compete in a knockout competition against the other provinces.

There has been a long-standing connection between the GAA and the Great Southern and Western Railway Company. In 1913 the Railway Company offered the GAA two trophies for the All-Ireland hurling and football championships.

The trophies were to become the absolute property of the first team to win two All-Ireland championships in a row. Kerry won the All-Ireland Football championships in 1913 and 1914 and thus they were presented with the 'first' Great Southern and Western Railway Trophy. In 1915 the company donated a new football trophy to the Association; again the trophy would be won outright by the team winning back-to-back All-Ireland championships. Wexford won the All-Ireland football championships in 1915 and 1916 and were accordingly awarded the 'second' Great Southern and Western Railway Trophy.

In 1925 the Great Southern and Western Railway was amalgamated with all the other railways operating wholly within the Irish Free State to form the Great Southern Railways. Cross-border railways were excluded from the merger. Two silver cups and two sets of gold medals were donated to the GAA by the Great Southern Railways and a decision was taken by Central Council to use these for the interprovincial competitions.

In the 1950s and 1960s the competitions were very popular, drawing large crowds of spectators. The final used to be played on St Patrick's Day, but since the 1980s the competition has been played in winter or in early spring.

GREAT SOUTHERN AND WESTERN RAILWAY
route map from around 1902.

International Fixtures

International Rules

The similarities between Gaelic football and Australian Rules football have long been

acknowledged. Since 1967 Irish teams have, intermittently, played Australian teams in Gaelic football, Compromise Rules and International Rules competitions.

The concept of the current International Rules series originates in the Australian

THE IRELAND INTERNATIONAL Rules team in Croke Park, 2016.

Football World Tour, which took place in 1967. The first series took place in Ireland in 1984 under a three-match format, whereby the team accumulating the most wins from the series was victorious.

The current International Rules competition sees the Irish and Australian sides compete for the Cormac McAnallen Cup.

Hurling/Shinty

Irish hurling teams faced their Scottish shinty playing counterparts at the Tailteann Games between 1924 and 1932. Shinty is a sport with very similar characteristics to hurling, played in the highlands of Scotland. Another series of matches in the same vein lapsed, but was revived in 1988 at Inverness under a set of hybrid rules, and continues to be played annually.

THE CORMAC MCANALLEN CUP.

Féile na nGael and Féile Peil na nÓg

Féile na nGael and Féile Peil na nÓg are the All-Ireland club festivals for hurling, Gaelic football, camogie, ladies football and handball for players under 14 years of age.

GAA FÉILE PEIL NA nÓg final 2010, Celtic Park, Derry.

The aim of Féile is to promote a philosophy whereby every player has the opportunity to participate and play in their respective Féile tournament at a level that is commensurate with their age, skills and strengths. Each county nominates teams to represent it at the national finals of Féile na nGael and Féile Peil na nÓg for hurling, camogie, Gaelic football, ladies football and handball.

GAA Online and GAAGO

SHANE LOWRY,
one of GAAGO's
many fans.

GAA Online

As with all modern sports reporting, the media coverage and analysis of Gaelic games has moved online. The impact of this online coverage means that information is now immediate and reaches wide and varied audiences instantly. Through social media channels such as Twitter and Facebook, fans have also become analysts and can offer their opinions in real time to online communities. They can also speak directly to their GAA heroes. Similarly, the GAA can communicate directly with fans via its website, as well as through dedicated Twitter (@officialgaa), Facebook and other social media accounts.

One of the most beneficial uses of online sports coverage is the timely way in which match results and team news can be communicated to supporters. A GAA fan on the other side of the world can find out the result of his or her local club's latest game within seconds of the final whistle! In the same vein, broadcasting rights packages now include deals to show Gaelic games online, which means that fans across the globe can watch live coverage of crucial GAA matches. The arrival of GAAGO on the broadcasting scene has been one of the most significant advances in the GAA's online development.

GAAGO

GAAGO is an online streaming service for Gaelic games outside Ireland. The service streams over 45 GAA football and hurling senior championship matches worldwide during the summer months and it also covers the closing stages of the GAA minor championships and the GAA under-21 hurling final. The GAA operates GAAGO in partnership with RTÉ, and the popular *Sunday Game* television programme is also available live as part of the GAAGO package.

Those subscribing to GAAGO have the option to pay per match or to purchase a season pass, and games can be watched on phones, tablets and laptops. In June 2015, Etihad Airways was announced as sponsor of GAAGO.

GAAGO has proved popular with Irish ex-pats as well as those travelling the world. Offaly golfer Shane Lowry is one such fan and has tweeted about his reliance on GAAGO to follow the Gaelic games season.

DUBLIN HURLER
Ryan O'Dwyer at the launch of GAAGO.

Media Personalities

The popularity of Gaelic games is reflected in the amount of Irish media coverage dedicated to the sports.

Across all channels – press, radio, television and online – there are endless previews, reviews, interviews and features reflecting on GAA matches, players and personalities.

The talented journalists who bring the games to life for fans often become GAA stars in their own right. Names such as Con Houlihan, Michael Lyster, Marty Morrissey, Des Cahill and Seán Óg Ó Ceallacháin are all synonymous with Gaelic games, but two men – Mícheál O'Hehir and Mícheál Ó Muircheartaigh – have become all-time GAA legends.

GAA BROADCASTER
Marty Morrissey.

Mícheál O'Hehir

'Thanks for the Memories.' This is how Gaelic games broadcaster Mícheál O'Hehir finished his 1996

MICHAEL O'HEHIR
commentating for
RTÉ in 1982.

autobiography. In reality, it is the army of Gaelic games fans who were treated to his memorable match commentaries throughout his lengthy career who should be thanking O'Hehir. The colour, entertainment and passion that his instantly recognisable voice brought into homes across Ireland will forever be remembered in the GAA community and beyond. His vivid descriptions of what was taking place on the field converted many to a lifelong love of the GAA.

O'Hehir's career began in 1938 following an audition for Radio Éireann. He was just 17 and still attending O'Connell's Secondary School in Dublin but he had been fascinated by the 'wireless' since early childhood. His audition was during a national football league game between Louth and Wexford where O'Hehir covered the second half of the match. That commentary was the start of a career that would span the next 47 years, and the man from Glasnevin would become known as 'The Voice of the GAA'.

During his time at the microphone, Mícheál commentated on 47 All-Ireland hurling finals and 52 All-Ireland football finals, clocking up a grand total of 99 All-Ireland finals at the microphone across radio and television. Unfortunately, he fell ill shortly before he achieved his 100th final, and he passed away in 1996 just a couple of weeks after a tribute night was held in his honour.

O'Hehir was also known for his exciting horse-racing commentaries, particularly for the Aintree Grand National, as well as for providing the voice for All-Ireland camogie finals. Other notable occasions when the Irish public heard his familiar tones included the official state visit by US president John F. Kennedy to Ireland and JFK's funeral just five months later. Mícheál was located in the NBC studios in New York for the funeral commentary and impressed his American colleagues so much with his handling of the coverage that he was offered a full-time job with ABC Television. Once again, for the state funeral of Roger Casement in 1965, it was the voice of Mícheál O'Hehir that covered events for television.

Of all of these career highlights, O'Hehir's most memorable commentary was for the 1947 All-Ireland senior football final from the Polo Grounds in New York. This was the first and only time that an All-Ireland final was played outside Ireland. The match, between Cavan and Kerry, was in the closing stages, when it seemed that the radio commentary would be lost, because the reservation on the international telephone lines expired at 5.00 pm.

Kerry were slow to come back on the field at the start of the second half so it began later than planned, and the final whistle was now due after 5.00 pm. Live on air, O'Hehir pleaded with the telephone exchange to give him five minutes more so Irish listeners could hear the result.

His wish was granted and Ireland heard Cavan win the game! In his autobiography O'Hehir wrote: 'I knew it would knock the bottom out of a great occasion if people in Ireland didn't hear the end of the match. If that happened I'm not sure I would have come home – well, maybe in disguise!'

With such a remarkable career, it's no wonder the legend of Mícheál O'Hehir lives on. In 2009, his name appeared at No.2 in the *Sunday Tribune* list of the 125 most influential people in GAA history, just one place behind founder Michael Cusack. The press and media centre in Croke Park is also named in his honour.

Mícheál Ó Muircheartaigh

One man who certainly regarded Mícheál O'Hehir as a hero was Mícheál Ó Muircheartaigh, who would himself go on to become one of the most famous voices in the history of Gaelic games. The man from Dingle (An Daingean) in County Kerry became known for his unique take on match events and for his humorous, yet accurate, descriptions of the play. Some of his most famous lines include:

MÍCHEÁL Ó MUIRCHEARTAIGH.

'He grabs the sliotar, he's on the 50 … , he's on the 40 … , he's on the 30 … , he's on the ground.'

'The stopwatch has stopped. It's up to God and the referee now. The referee is Pat Horan. God is God.'

'Pat Fox has it on the hurl … he's motoring well now … but here comes Joe Rabbitte hot on his tail … I've seen it all now, a Rabbitte chasing a Fox around Croke Park.'

'Teddy McCarthy to John McCarthy, no relation. John McCarthy back to Teddy McCarthy, still no relation.'

'Seán Óg Ó hAilpín … his father's from Fermanagh, his mother's from Fiji, neither one a hurling stronghold.'

Ó Muircheartaigh's career across radio and television in both the English and Irish languages lasted from 1949 to 2010. His first broadcast came from Croke Park on St Patrick's Day 1949 when he was just 18 years old. His final commentary also came from GAA headquarters 62 years later, when he was at the microphone for the radio coverage of the final test between Australia and Ireland in the 2010 International Rules series.

Did you know?

The first live radio broadcast of a field sports game outside the US was for a hurling game. P. D. Mehigan commentated on the All-Ireland hurling semi-final between Kilkenny and Galway for 2RN (Ireland's first radio station) on 29 August 1926.

GAA – A Global Phenomenon

Wherever Irish people have settled in large numbers, Gaelic games have been organised.

The first game played under GAA rules outside Ireland took place on Boston Common in 1886, just two years after the Association was founded. Today the GAA continues to serve as a focus for the Irish community throughout the world. From its traditional international strongholds of Britain and America, the GAA has spread further afield in recent decades. There are now more international clubs than ever and, as the games are played in more and more countries, the GAA has become a global phenomenon.

Britain

Gaelic games have been played in Britain since the late 18th century. The first club to be established there was the Hibernian Athletic Club in London, formed in 1895. The London County Board was

LONDON JERSEYS
in the dressing room.

established in 1896 and key figures included Liam MacCarthy and Sam Maguire, who would both lend their names to the All-Ireland championship trophies. Between 1900 and 1908, London competed in nine All-Ireland finals and won the 1901 hurling title. The Provincial Council of Britain was established in 1926 and remains the only GAA council outside Ireland with provincial status.

CHILDREN PLAYING
Gaelic football in San Francisco.

The US

The early history of the GAA in North America centres around New York, where the first real attempt to organise Gaelic games came in 1891. It wasn't until 1914 that the Gaelic Athletic Association of New York was founded – club competitions in hurling and football have been taking place there since 1915. During the 1950s GAA boards were established in other areas, and in 1959 the North American Board was formed to promote and control Gaelic games across the US. Gaelic games are currently organised and played in over 40 cities across North America. Clubs take part in divisional championship competitions to qualify for the North American final.

Europe
The rise of Gaelic games in regions beyond Britain and the US has been a singular feature of the Association's international development since the mid-1990s. The visa-free movement of people in the European Union has been an important contributory factor in this development, and Gaelic games in Europe are expanding and developing at a rapid rate. The longest established European club is Luxembourg GAA, which was founded in 1978, and in 1999 the European Board was set up. This board now has over 50 affiliated clubs across more than 20 countries, and covers diverse languages and regional dialects including Breton, Catalan and Galician. Both camogie and ladies football also continue to develop at a European level.

MARY MOLLY O'ROURKE

of New York in action in Croke Park.

Australasia

The Australasian Board of the GAA promotes Gaelic games in nine regions throughout Australia and New Zealand. While forms of Gaelic games have been played in Australia since the 19th century, it wasn't until the 1960s that local associations were formed. In 1974, the Gaelic Athletic Association of Australia was formed to promote Gaelic games on a national level. With the later affiliation of Auckland and Wellington, the name was changed to the Gaelic Athletic Association of Australasia. With the recent surge in emigration to the region, the Australasian Board has a record number of registered players.

Canada

Gaelic games have been played in Canada since the 19th century when the first Irish immigrants arrived. In 1845, a by-law passed in Sillery, Quebec, forbade hurling in the town's narrow streets! It wasn't until the 1950s and 1960s that Gaelic games were formalised throughout Canada. Many of the clubs that exist today were founded during this period.

Asia and the Gulf Region

A new development of the GAA since the 1990s is the establishment of clubs in Asia and the Gulf region. In 2012, the Asian County Board was renamed the Asian Gulf Board and it currently has an affiliation of almost 30 clubs across 16 countries. The annual Asian Gaelic Games tournament has developed rapidly since 1996. The tournament moves to a different Asian city each year. It is the premium Irish event and the largest amateur team event in the region.

Argentina

The earliest reference to hurling in Argentina is from the late 1880s in the ranching town of Mercedes, Buenos Aires, a major hub of the Irish-Argentine community. The Argentine Hurling Club was formed in 1900 and the first official game was played on 15 July. Games were played weekly until 1914 and received local media coverage. The outbreak of World War I made it almost impossible to import hurleys from Ireland and the native Argentine mountain ash was too heavy and inflexible. Although the game was revived after the end of the war, the golden age of Argentine hurling had passed.

The Artane Band

The distinctive scarlet and blue uniforms of the Artane Band are a much-loved sight in Croke Park on big match days.

THE ARTANE BAND
in Croke Park
in 2011.

The Artane Band, originally called the Artane Boys Band, was founded in 1872 by Brother Alphonsus Hoope, Superior of the Artane Industrial School. The band gave its first performance for Edward VII, then Prince of Wales, in the grounds of the school on the north side of Dublin.

The relationship between the marching band and the Gaelic Athletic Association began in 1886 when the fledgeling GAA invited it to play at the Whit Monday games at the North Circular Road grounds. This link has endured throughout the years and the band accompanied the Kerry and Cavan teams to New York in 1947 when the All-Ireland senior football final was played at the Polo Grounds, on the only occasion that the All-Ireland finals have taken place outside of Ireland.

Nowadays, the Artane Band is a constant presence in Croke Park during the GAA All-Ireland football and hurling championship season. It performs the national anthem on the pitch before games and entertains the crowds at half-time.

The Artane Band is known internationally and it has performed for world leaders, including US presidents Kennedy, Nixon and Clinton, as well as Her Majesty Queen Elizabeth II of Britain during her visit to Croke Park in 2011. Along the way, the band has launched some notable music careers, including that of Larry Mullen, the drummer from U2. Interestingly, a photograph of three band members in full uniform is featured on the cover of the INXS rock album *Welcome to Wherever You Are*, released in 1992.

AVA JOHNSTON, one of the first ever female drum majors to lead the Artane Band, in Semple Stadium in 2015.

Fans and Big Match Days

GAA matches are full of colour and noise and the air is brimming with excitement.

FERMANAGH SUPPORTERS.

Clothing

GAA fans are known for their loyalty to their team, and most people are wearing their team colours – either a jersey or a headband. A feature of the games are the headband sellers that assemble around the grounds for supporters who want to add some last-minute colour to their outfit.

In 1991 sponsors were included on jerseys for the first time. One of the only remaining sponsors from this time is Carroll Meats, who still sponsor Offaly.

Wearing an older or vintage jersey is quite common. The style and design of the jersey may change, but the county colours remain the same.

Match programmes

A supporter's visit to a game is not complete without a match programme. The details of the team's starting line-up, news from the team and advertising for companies that support the GAA are contained in the programme. It is also a souvenir of the day out at the game. GAA programmes are collectors' items, and many sell at auction for large sums.

Pageantry

On big match days, there is a hive of activity wherever you look. Volunteer stewards are directing supporters to their seats. Journalists are conducting interviews for radio and TV broadcasts.

A guard of honour greets the team as they run on to the pitch. The trophy is on a podium as the players run out of the tunnel. The players then line up to be presented to the president of Ireland.

MATCH PROGRAMME
cover for the 1961
All-Ireland senior
football final.

Before the game, the players often walk behind a band around the field, giving their supporters a chance to cheer them on before the match. Then the supporters and players stand for the national anthem, a solemn moment before the intensity of the game.

In Croke Park at the end of the game, the winning team make their

way up the steps of the Hogan
Stand to receive their trophy.
Afterwards they do a lap of honour
to show the silverware to their
supporters in the stands.

WESTMEATH
stand for the
national anthem.

ALAN MILTON, GAA HEAD OF COMMUNICATIONS, AND RAY MCMANUS of Sportsfile at the launch of *A Season of Sundays* in 2014.

A Season of Sundays

One of the best ways to capture the emotional highs and lows of the GAA All-Ireland championship season and beyond is through the photographer's lens.

Sports photographs have the unique capability of freezing a particular moment in time and recording the joy and disappointment of the winners and losers. Each year sports photography agency Sportsfile produces a collection of the best GAA photos of the season in a coffee-table book called *A Season of Sundays*.

This publication, which has been released every year since the 1990s, provides an amazing photographic account of the GAA year that was. Each book, with images taken by a team of Sportsfile photographers, includes a range of photos from all levels of Gaelic games life. Pictures are included from local club matches with small attendances and from the full-house finals that play out in Croke Park, and from the dark days of winter to the high dramas of the summer. The faces featured include the players, managers, fans and the unsung behind-the-scenes heroes, while the accompanying text from award-winning sports writers really brings the season to life and jogs the memory. Books in *A Season of Sundays* series have now become collectors' items.

GAA on Screen – Television and Cinema

Since the arrival of television in Ireland, coverage of Gaelic games has been an important aspect of the programming schedule.

When Telefís Éireann opened for business in 1961, the idea of broadcasting coverage of Ireland's national sports was high on the agenda. The first match shown on Irish television screens was the Railway Cup hurling final of 1962, which was contested by Munster and Leinster on 17 March. Previously fans had been able to see highlights of important GAA matches on newsreels in cinemas. These images were filmed by the National Film Institute and footage still exists from the 1940s. Notably, the BBC showed highlights of the All-Ireland senior hurling final as far back as 1959.

Initially the GAA was cautious of the live television broadcasts and it restricted television

RTÉ RADIO AND TELEVISION
presenter Des Cahill.

coverage to the All-Ireland senior finals, the two
semi-finals and the Railway Cup finals in both
hurling and football. In 1971, the first match to
be broadcast in colour was the All-Ireland senior
hurling final between Tipperary and Kilkenny.

A VIEW
of the media facilities
at Croke Park.

Through the
decades, television
coverage of Gaelic
games has constantly
diversified, with more
broadcasters coming
on board and matches
now being shown on
TV screens all over the
world and in HD. Irish
television networks
RTÉ, TG4, TV3, BBC

Northern Ireland and Setanta Sports have all
covered live Gaelic games, and in 2014 Sky Sports
also entered the arena, securing exclusive island-

THE SKY SPORTS TEAM

in Croke Park in 2014.

of-Ireland rights to 14 championship games. Television coverage no longer stops with the final whistle and GAA broadcasts now include preview and review programmes as well as opinion and analysis from journalists and former GAA stars.

The GAA media rights deal covering the period 2014 to 2017 recognises the importance of broadcasting Gaelic games to those living outside Ireland. Sky Sports now broadcasts live coverage of games in Britain, while Australian network Channel 7 shows live coverage of all 45 championship games free to air.

Gaelic games have also had an impact on popular culture, featuring on both television and film screens. Director Ken Loach's award-winning 2006 film *The Wind that Shakes the Barley* opens with a sequence from a hurling match in Cork, while the 1958 film *Rooney*, starring John Gregson, depicts the life of a GAA player. The filmmakers were given permission for Gregson to run on to the Croke Park pitch ahead of the two teams in the 1957 All-Ireland senior hurling final between Kilkenny and Waterford. Gregson wore a Kilkenny jersey for the occasion!

TG4'S JULIET MURPHY AND GRÁINNE MCELWAIN in Croke Park in 2014.

GAA Grounds

Croke Park

Croke Park is the home of the GAA and it has been at the heart of Irish sporting life for over a hundred years.

It is a modern stadium that is one of the largest in Europe with a capacity of 82,300. It is located on the north side of Dublin, just outside the hustle and bustle of the city centre.

AN AERIAL VIEW of the modern Croke Park.

Each year there are at least 30 match days in the stadium, usually two matches per day. Teams from football, hurling, camogie and ladies football, playing mainly inter-county matches, compete in Croke Park. Days are set aside each year for children from around the country to travel to Croke Park to play on the pitch.

The Early Years

In 1908 Frank Dineen purchased the Jones's Road grounds from City and Suburban Racecourse and Amusements Grounds Ltd and in 1913 the grounds were purchased by the GAA. The name of the grounds was changed to Croke Park in honour of Archbishop Thomas Croke, who was the first patron of the GAA.

The GAA sought to improve standards for spectators at their new venue. The first job was to create a standing terrace, which became known as Hill 16. It was said to have been created out of rubble

THE STEEL FRAME of the new Cusack Stand, 1938.

PROGRAMME COVER

for the opening of the new Hogan Stand, 1959.

from Sackville Street, now O'Connell Street, left after the 1916 Rising. However, it is also possible that the name Hill 16 comes from Hill 60, where Irish fusiliers fought during World War I in Gallipoli.

In preparation for the Tailteann Games, a new stand was built and opened in 1924. This stand was subsequently named the Hogan Stand, in honour of Michael Hogan, the Tipperary player who was shot dead in Croke Park on Bloody Sunday. The Hogan Stand was demolished and a new stand, of the same name, was built in its place in 1959. In 1938 the Cusack Stand, named in honour of the founder Michael Cusack, was officially opened – this stand underwent significant modifications in 1966.

Finally a small stand was erected next to Hill 16, called the Nally Stand in acknowledgment of the contribution made by Patrick Nally, who gave great support to Michael Cusack in the lead-up to the inaugural Thurles meeting.

Modern Redevelopment

In the late 1980s it was agreed that a new modern stadium was required as the current grounds wouldn't be suitable for the future generations of supporters. The GAA set about a programme of redevelopment works that would take 12 years to complete.

THE NEW CUSACK STAND being built in 1993.

During that time, Croke Park was redeveloped stand by stand, without causing any disruption to the staging of matches in the grounds.

Cusack Stand – Work began in 1993 and the new modern stand was completed in 1995.

Canal End – The terrace was removed and replaced with a new stand, named the *Davin Stand* (after Maurice Davin, first president of the GAA) by Seán Kelly, president of the GAA at the time.

Hogan Stand – The new stand was fitted with a modern media centre and a VIP area for special guests. It was ready in time for the 2002 All-Ireland finals.

Dineen Hill 16 and Nally Stand – In 2003 work began on upgrading these into modern terraces. The Nally Stand became a terrace, and Frank Dineen was honoured by having Hill 16 named after him.

The completed stadium was officially opened in March 2005 by Taoiseach Bertie Ahern.

There have been further enhancement to the grounds since 2005. Two large screens were installed in the bowl and floodlights were installed in 2005.

The Pitch

The pitch in Croke Park Stadium is considered one of the finest in the world. The total size is 15,000m^2. The pitch is 144 metres long and 88 metres wide. An under-soil heating system and drainage network ensure that the playing surface can be kept in pristine

THE ARTIFICIAL LIGHTS
that are used in the winter months in Croke Park to help the grass grow.

THE GAA MUSEUM,
Croke Park.

condition even in winter. Artificial lights are used in winter to help the growth of the grass.

The GAA Museum – Cultural, Social and Sporting Heritage

The GAA Museum is the home of the national GAA collections and archive. It celebrates the contribution that the GAA has made to cultural, social and sporting life in Ireland.

Over the past 17 years, the GAA Museum has become one of the most popular visitor attractions in the capital and is

THE GAA
MUSEUM'S
Club Wall.

now ranked as one of the top three museums to visit in Dublin. It is a fully accredited museum, one of only a few in Ireland.

The museum's exhibition galleries extend across two floors and vividly illustrate the history and development of Gaelic games from ancient times to the present day. It showcases a diverse collection of objects representing the rich 131-year history of the Association. The collection includes minute books from Geraldine's in London when Michael Collins was secretary, the original Sam Maguire and Liam McCarthy trophies and the Jack Lynch, Christy Ring and Jimmy Doyle medal collections.

The museum is also home to GAA-related exhibitions, including the GAA Hall of Fame, the Treasury of Trophies and memorabilia of modern-day football and hurling heroes.

The entrance to the museum is the location of the GAA Club Wall, on which are shown the crests of all the GAA clubs. It was unveiled in 2009 to celebrate the 125th anniversary of the Association. It is a popular post for photos in Croke Park.

The GAA Museum run regular tours of the stadium. In 2012 a new tour was opened – on the rooftop of Croke Park! The Etihad Skyline tour is a walkway around the three stands and it gives visitor the opportunity to enjoy panoramic views of Dublin city from 17 storeys above ground level.

THE ETIHAD SKYLINE TOUR
A view of the rooftop walkway.

THE CROKE PARK HOTEL.

The Croke Park Hotel

Opened in 2005, this four-star hotel is located directly across from Croke Park on Jones's Road. It hosts many GAA functions, and it also works with the Croke Park meetings and events team on conference business. The hotel is always a hive of activity before and after matches in Croke Park.

Concerts

Over the years, Croke Park has hosted some very famous concerts for some of the world's largest acts in the music industry.

   From Neil Diamond to Celine Dion, U2 to Bon Jovi, One Direction to Ed Sheeran, they have all performed to sell-out crowds of 82,000 people. It is a great added dimension to the stadium.

U2 AND NEIL DIAMOND are some of the major acts that have performed in Croke Park.

MATCH PROGRAMME cover for the American football game that was held in Croke Park in 1953.

American Football in Croke Park

Ties between Ireland and the US mean that close links have also developed between Irish sports and American sports.

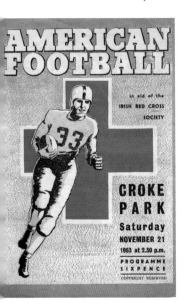

GAA clubs have sprung up across the US as a result of emigration, while interest and enthusiasm for US games has grown Ireland. With this in mind, it's notable that Croke Park has played host to a number of American football games.

US Servicemen 1953

In August 1953, the Irish Red Cross was granted permission by the GAA Central Council to fundraise by staging a game of American football between two American teams in Croke Park. The game between the Burtonwood Bullets and the Wethersfield

Raiders took place at 2.30 pm on 21 November 1953
before a crowd of 40,000. The game was the final of
the American Air-Force League and both teams were
London-based, made up of US servicemen stationed
in Britain. Irish president Seán T. O'Kelly attended
the game, along with the papal nuncio and the
American ambassador.

Shamrock Classic 1996

In November 1996, US Naval Academy (Navy) and
Notre Dame began a new competition called the
Shamrock Classic. The Colleges game was played in
Croke Park, with Notre Dame beating Navy 54–27.
Approximately 40,000 people attended this game
with an estimated 10,000 fans travelling from the US
for the encounter.

American Bowl 1997

On 27 July 1997 the first NFL (National Football
League) game to be played in Ireland took place

**PITTSBURGH
STEELERS V
CHICAGO BEARS**
in Croke Park, 1997.

CHEERLEADERS
with the Dan
Rooney Trophy in
Croke Park in 2014.

in Croke Park as the Chicago Bears faced the
Pittsburgh Steelers. Temporary floodlighting was
installed in the stadium for the occasion. Steelers
president Dan Rooney, a high-profile name on the
Irish-American scene, was influential in bringing
the game to Ireland. On the day, the Steelers beat the
Bears 30-17 in front of a crowd of 36,000.

Croke Park Classic 2014

The Croke Park Classic saw the University of Central
Florida (UCF) host Penn State University in the
2014 American College Football Season Opener,
playing for the Dan Rooney Trophy at Croke Park
on 30 August 2014. This big season opener for UCF
and Penn State was the first time that the teams
had played outside the US. American football
fans travelled to Ireland in their thousands for the
occasion and the game was played in front of a crowd
of 53,304. The Temple Bar area in Dublin's city centre
was transformed into a Croke Park Classic 'fanzone',

with crowds attending pep rallies for both teams. The game itself was an exciting one with drama in the closing moments. Penn State were the victors after player Sam Ficken scored a field goal in the last seconds of the match. The final score was Penn State 26–UCF 24.

THE PENN STATE UNIVERSITY TEAM on the Etihad Skyline, Croke Park, in 2014.

Famous Visitors to Croke Park

As the headquarters of the Gaelic Athletic Association, Croke Park has seen some famous players grace the pitch over the years. However, Ireland's most iconic sports arena has lured more than just sports stars north of the River Liffey.

PRINCESS GRACE OF MONACO
in Croke Park
in 1961.

The stadium on Jones's Road has welcomed royalty, international dignitaries and even an astronaut onto its hallowed turf.

Princess Grace

In 1961, Princess Grace of Monaco visited Croke Park when she accompanied her husband, Prince Rainier, to Dublin for the opening ceremony of the Dublin International Festival of Music and Arts. The royal couple were in attendance because the National Operatic Orchestra of Monaco was participating in the event.

President of the People's Republic of China

Chinese Premier Xi Jinping tested his Gaelic football and hurling skills while visiting Croke Park in 2012, as captured in this iconic photograph. Mr Xi toured the stadium with the Irish ambassador to China, Declan Kelleher, and Beijing GAA men's team captain Enda Winters. Mr Xi spent three days in Ireland, where he also visited the Cliffs of Moher and a dairy farm in County Clare.

Her Majesty Queen Elizabeth II

The historic visit of Britain's Queen Elizabeth II and the Duke of Edinburgh to Croke Park took place on 18 May 2011 as part of a state visit to Ireland, the first by a British monarch since 1911. The stopover at Croke Park was of particular significance in light of the events of Bloody Sunday 1920.

GAA president Christy Cooney welcomed the Queen on behalf of members of the GAA throughout Ireland and across the world before

CHINESE PREMIER XI JINGPING tries his hand with hurling in Croke Park in 2012.

providing a tour of the stadium where the couple visited the dressing rooms and the famous pitch. Her Majesty was presented with a book entitled *The GAA: A People's History*, while the Duke received a hurley and sliotar.

QUEEN ELIZABETH II
of Britain visits Croke
Park in 2011.

Commander Chris Hadfield

Chris Hadfield, the first Canadian to walk in space, also walked in Croke Park! The decorated astronaut was another visitor to try his hand at the ancient sport of hurling during his trip and he also spent time examining the trophy collection in the GAA Museum.

Commander Hadfield became an instant hit in Ireland when he sent the first tweet from space in the Irish language during his time at the International Space Station. His trip to Croke Park took place in January 2014 following his return to earth.

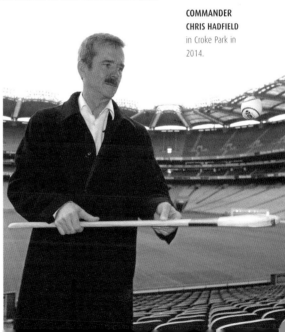

COMMANDER CHRIS HADFIELD in Croke Park in 2014.

Muhammad Ali Fight, Croke Park 1972

While All-Ireland finals are the biggest annual sporting occasions in Croke Park, other memorable events have taken place in the stadium.

MATCH PROGRAMME cover for the Muhammad Ali v Al Blue Lewis fight held in Croke Park in 1972.

One of the most notable is the fight between boxing icon Muhammad Ali and Al 'Blue' Lewis, which played out in front of a boisterous crowd on 19 July 1972.

INTERNATIONAL HEAVYWEIGHT CONTEST

MUHAMMAD ALI

AL BLUE LEWIS

CROKE PARK, DUBLIN
WEDNESDAY, 19th JULY, 1972

PROGRAMME

There was huge interest in the fight amongst Irish media and sports fans, with lots of hype surrounding the build-up. The fight took place soon after Ali's boxing licence was returned. It had been taken away after his opposition to the Vietnam War and his conviction for draft evasion.

Ali returned to the ring, losing to Joe Frazier in 'The Fight of the

Century' in 1971, registering his first professional defeat. He then embarked on a world tour, fighting 13 times in six countries before his famous rematch against Frazier in 1974. Croke Park was one of his stops and he immediately endeared himself to the Irish public when he landed at Dublin Airport and declared he had Irish ancestors. This proved to be correct, as Ali's maternal great-grandfather Abe Grady was born in County Clare and emigrated to America in the 1860s.

While Ali did not appear to rate Lewis's chances in his pre-fight interviews, the fight did go to the 11th round before Ali won on technical knockout (TKO).

A SELECTION OF ARTEFACTS from the Ali v Lewis fight on display in the GAA Museum.

Ali returned to Croke Park in 2003 for the opening ceremony of the Special Olympics and he came to Ireland again in 2009 when he visited Ennis, the birthplace of Abe Grady. He was made an honorary freeman of the town.

A full account of Ali's time in Ireland and Michael 'Butty' Sugrue's efforts to bring the fight to Croke Park can be seen in the documentary *When Ali Came to Ireland*, directed by Ross Whitaker. A signed Muhammad Ali boxing glove and the shorts he wore for the Croke Park fight are on display in the GAA Museum.

MUHAMMAD ALI
visiting Croke Park in 2003.

The Olympic Torch Comes to Croke Park

On the morning of 6 June 2012, the Olympic Flame arrived at Croke Park as part of the 2012 Summer Olympics Torch Relay.

The relay, which took place in advance of the London Games, lasted 70 days, with over 8,000 people carrying the torch over 8,000 miles. The Olympic Flame's visit to Dublin was on Day 19 of the torch run.

Kilkenny hurling legend Henry Shefflin was given the honour of carrying the torch around Croke Park, and the main part of the route saw him walk on the

HENRY SHEFFLIN
with the Olympic Torch in Croke Park in 2012.

HENRY SHEFFLIN AND RONNIE DELANY at the unveiling of the Olympic Flame statue on the Etihad Skyline, 2015.

Etihad Skyline walkway on the roof of the stadium.

In September 2015, a new sculpture of the Olympic Flame was unveiled on the Etihad Skyline to mark its 2012 visit to Croke Park. The sculpture includes a plaque recognising the record-breaking achievements of Henry Shefflin.

Semple Stadium

Located in Thurles, County Tipperary, this is
the main GAA ground for the Munster region.
Founded in 1910, it has a capacity of 53,000,
making it one of the largest stadiums in Ireland.

**THE 1908
TIPPERARY
TEAM**
Tom Semple is
seated in the
front row, fourth
from the left.

In 1971 the grounds were named after Thomas Semple,
a famous hurler for the Old Thurles Blues. He won All-
Irelands with Tipperary in 1900, 1906 and 1908.

The Dr Kinane Stand and Ardán Ó Riain were named after two clergymen. Dr Kinane was archbishop of Cashel and GAA patron for 13 years. Canon M.K. Ryan played a key role in the purchase of the land that became Semple Stadium.

In 2009 upgrade works on Semple Stadium were completed ahead of the GAA 125th anniversary celebration. They included the installation of floodlights, provision of corporate and VIP facilities, and upgrading of the terraces and irrigation.

THE 2015 MUNSTER SENIOR HURLING FINAL between Waterford and Tipperary, Semple Stadium. ·

Gaelic Games pre-1884

While the GAA was founded in 1884 with the aims of controlling Irish athletics and reviving hurling and Gaelic football, the games themselves were played in Ireland long before the GAA was established.

Hurling has been played in Ireland since mythological times: according to Irish legend the first battle of Moytura (1272 BC) was preceded by a 27-a-side game of hurling between the warring factions, the Firbolg and the Tuatha de Dannan. The boy Setanta played with his hurl and sliotar as he travelled to Emain Mhaca, and while there he used them to kill the hound of Culainn before taking his place and name – Cúchulainn. Outside of mythology, hurling featured in the ancient Irish Brehon Laws, which contained provisions for compensation where death or injury were caused by a hurl or sliotar. From the 12th-century

1785 EYEWITNESS STATEMENT
about a fatal blow during a game a hurling.

Norman invasion, attempts were made by the invaders to persuade or force the Irish to stop playing the game, but it continued to be played. The 1367 parliament argued that the game of hurling led to the neglect of military duties, and in 1527 the Statute of Galway ordered loyal subjects not to participate in the game. Hurling, however, continued to flourish, and by the 1600s many of the Gaelic chieftains had their own paid hurling teams. While hurling was banned by the Sunday Observance Act of 1695, the game continued to be played for the next 150 years, until the advent of the famine, and frequent references to the game can be found in memoirs, poems, newspaper reports and local lore.

While not as numerous, there are some references to some sort of football being played in Ireland since the Middle Ages. It is not until the 17th and 18th centuries, however, that references to a uniquely Irish code of football can be identified; for example,

1784 POEM
entitled 'The Hurling Ball'.

a poem published in Dublin in 1722 tells of a football match near the Phoenix Park between teams from Swords and Lusk, during which the ball was thrown and kicked, and wrestling was permitted. Newspapers from the early 19th century carry frequent reports of games being staged throughout Ireland, right up until the time of the famine.

The Irish famine of 1847, while being a humanitarian crisis, was also a watershed in the social history of Ireland. Among the victims of the famine were the field games and other traditional pastimes of rural Ireland. However, while the games declined dramatically, they did not die out completely – between the ending of the famine and the establishment of the GAA, there are some references to the games. Michael Cusack, the founder of the GAA, later wrote that he had seen hurling played in north Clare and south Galway as a boy in the 1850s, while there is also evidence that football continued to be played in Tipperary, Cork, Kerry and Limerick. The growing popularity of cricket in Ireland, however, posed the greatest threat to the indigenous games.

It was not until the formation of the Gaelic Athletic Association in 1884 that the native pastimes were codified and controlled by one administrative body.

Michael Cusack

Michael Cusack is frequently, and rightly, credited as the founder of the Gaelic Athletic Association.

Cusack was born in Carron, County Clare on 20 September 1847; both of his parents died at a relatively young age. Cusack married Margaret Woods in June 1876 and they had six children. He died unexpectedly on 28 November 1906, four months short of his 60th birthday.

A qualified teacher, in 1877 Cusack set up his own successful academy in Dublin to prepare students for civil and public service entrance examinations. Sport was central to the everyday life of students in the school.

While Cusack was an active participant in rugby, cricket and athletics, from mid-1882, he turned his attentions to the revival of hurling. In December 1882 he formed the Dublin Hurling Club, whose aim was to '[take] steps to

MICHAEL CUSACK.

re-establish the national game of hurling'. The Dublin Hurling Club lasted only two months, folding in late February 1883, but Cusack persevered and continued playing hurling in the Phoenix Park on Saturday afternoons. By October 1883, the number of people playing alongside Cusack had increased to such an extent that the Cusack's Academy Hurling Club was formed. This hurling club, in turn, led to the establishment of the Metropolitan Hurling Club – Cusack later wrote that it was the Metropolitan Hurling Club 'out of which the GAA sprang'.

Cusack's other great passion, in addition to sport, was journalism. Beginning in 1880,

Cusack was a regular contributor to newspapers as a letter-writer, columnist, reporter, editor and owner.

Cusack used newspapers to further his aims of establishing an indigenous athletics body in Ireland: on 11 October 1884 the nationalist *United Ireland* newspaper published Cusack's epistle 'A Word About Irish Athletics', while *United Ireland*, *The Freeman's Journal* and *The Irishman* were all used by Cusack to the advantage of the GAA in the lead-up and aftermath of the 1 November 1884 foundation meeting.

Following the establishment of the GAA in 1884, Cusack secured a weekly column in *United Ireland*. He used this to great effect to publicise and popularise the fledgeling GAA.

The period between the founding of the GAA and 1886 was one of immense growth and development and, by the end of 1885, the GAA was well organised in 20 of the 32 counties.

Cusack worked tirelessly to ensure the growth of the association he had founded: in addition to running Cusack's Academy and writing a regular column for *United Ireland*, he attended four provincial sports meetings during 1885, attended the three important indoor GAA athletic meetings in 1886 and

LETTER, DATED 26 AUGUST 1884,
from Michael Cusack to Maurice Davin,
organising the first meeting of the GAA.

attended some, but not all, of the GAA meetings held during 1885 and 1886.

In July 1886, however, only 20 months after its foundation, the GAA removed Cusack from the post of secretary.

By April 1886 there was friction between Cusack and other members of the GAA, and he unintentionally offended Archbishop Croke in a letter.

At a special meeting, held in Thurles on 4 July 1886, Cusack was accused of being negligent in answering letters, of having failed to keep accounts and of having been offensive to anybody who dared disagree with him. When the votes were counted, it was revealed that the majority of the GAA had decided that it was time for Cusack to part company with the organisation he had founded.

Worse was still to come for Cusack – in August 1886, the owner of *United Ireland*, William O'Brien, removed Cusack as a columnist. Cusack then established his own short-lived newspaper, *The Celtic Times*.

This, however, was not the end of Cusack's involvement with the GAA. In March 1893 he was controversially elected secretary of the Dublin County Board, but his dictatorial style of leadership meant that by the summer, two-thirds of the Dublin clubs had withdrawn their affiliation from the board and vowed not to return while Cusack remained as secretary.

When the GAA Central Council ruled that Cusack's election as secretary had been invalid, Cusack fought the decision every inch of the way, until he was eventually removed from power in October 1893.

In 1901, Cusack unsuccessfully stood as a candidate for secretary of the GAA; this marked his last involvement with the GAA.

COVER
from Michael Cusack's 1887
The Celtic Times newspaper.

The First All-Ireland Championships

THE TIPPERARY (THURLES) TEAM, winners of the first All-Ireland hurling championship.

While today's All-Ireland championships are the sporting events of the year, the first All-Ireland championships were very low-key, and were barely mentioned in the press at all.

The decision to hold an All-Ireland championship in 1887, in both hurling and football, was made by the GAA at their November 1886 Annual Convention. Five counties participated in the hurling championship with seven participating in the football competition. The open draw for both competitions was made on 27 February 1887.

For the 1887 championships (and until 1923), the winning club from each county was given the privilege of representing their county in the All-Ireland series.

The clubs that contested the 1887 hurling championship were Thurles (Tipperary), Meelick (Galway), Castlebridge (Wexford), Smith O'Briens (Clare) and Tullaroan (Kilkenny).

The clubs that contested the football championship were Dundalk Young Irelands (Louth), Ballyduff Lower (Waterford), Kilmacow (Kilkenny), Lees Club (Cork), Commercials (Limerick), Dowdstown (Meath) and Templemore (Tipperary).

Games in the championship were played by teams consisting of 21 players, on a pitch much larger than today's standard, while 'soccer-style' goal posts were used, with 'points posts' placed at either side of the goal posts. A goal outweighed any number of points while 'forfeit points' were awarded

LIMERICK COMMERCIALS, ALL-IRELAND CHAMPIONS, 1887.

THE LIMERICK (COMMERCIALS) TEAM, winners of the first All-Ireland football championship.

in place of today's 45s and 65s, with five forfeit points equalling one point.

In the hurling championship Tipperary got a walk-over from Dublin in the first round before defeating Clare and Kilkenny to reach the final.

Galway qualified for the final by defeating Wexford. At the final itself, held at Birr on 1 April 1888, Tipperary beat Galway on the score of 1-01 to nil. At this final, tree branches were used as goal posts. The Tipperary team turned up so late that the Galway men had begun to eat a meal at a nearby hotel. Only for the fact that so many had travelled by train to watch the game, it would have been cancelled.

In the football championship Limerick beat Meath and Kilkenny in the opening rounds, and then overcame Tipperary in the semi-final. The final of the competition, between Limerick and Louth, was played at Clonskeagh on 29 April 1888. Limerick won the game on the score of 1-04 to 0-03.

To get to Clonskeagh, the Limerick team travelled to Dublin by train the previous evening and on the day itself they took a horse tram to Ranelagh Avenue, where they changed to another horse tram, which brought them the remainder of their journey.

The medals for the first All-Ireland hurling and football champions were not presented to the players until 1913.

The 1887/1888 Split and Reconstruction

With legislative independence the burning issue of the day, keeping politics out of the GAA would have been impossible.

EDWARD BENNETT, president of the GAA in 1887.

The Irish Republican Brotherhood (IRB) infiltrated the GAA from an early stage, with the aim of using the Association to further their political ambitions. As its strength grew within the GAA, the IRB tried to introduce a series of rules, angering Maurice Davin so much that he resigned his presidency in April 1887.

The 1887 Convention was one of the most dramatic meetings in the history of the GAA. An estimated 800 people gathered in Thurles Courthouse for the meeting. Within minutes of the convention starting, a serious row broke out between supporters of the IRB and supporters of the Parnell's Irish National League as to who should chair the meeting. As the row intensified, fist fights broke out around the hall, with the leader of the National League faction, Fr Scanlan, leading his followers (around 200 men) to Hayes Hotel, where he declared his intention to form a new athletic association. Back in the courthouse, the convention elected Edward Bennett, the IRB candidate. The IRB felt confident that they had taken full control of the GAA.

The next day, Archbishop Croke wrote a letter to the *Freeman's Journal* disassociating himself from the IRB branch of the GAA. Over 250 clubs had registered their disapproval of the IRB-led executive within a fortnight. Following some conciliatory work by Croke and Davitt, the executive called for county conventions to be held by 27 December 1887, with a full annual convention planned for 4 January 1888.

At this convention, changes were made to the playing rules, but it was the elections of officers that was crucial. Maurice Davin was elected president, while his friend William Prendergast was elected secretary. Symbolically, the nationalist MP William O'Brien was invited to become a patron. While the IRB faction kept some positions of power, it was, in effect, ousted – the six-week split ended with a whimper; planning for the upcoming 1888 Invasion Tour helped unite and focus minds.

1888 Invasion Tour

One of the ideas considered by the founders of the GAA was the revival of the ancient Tailteann Games (An Aonach Tailteann).

SOME OF THE ATHLETES
that travelled to America in 1888.

In 1888 the idea of hosting a Celtic festival was raised and plans were made to hold it in Dublin in the summer of 1889. The festival would include

field games, athletic contests, an industrial exhibition and literary and musical competitions. It was estimated that hosting the festival would cost £5,000. To raise this amount it was planned that a group of Irish athletes would embark on a fundraising tour of Irish centres in the US, staging displays of hurling and athletics and international contests between Ireland and the US.

£1,000 would be needed for this tour and a nationwide fundraising campaign was initiated. In the meantime, the process of selecting hurlers and athletes to go on the tour began.

When the Central Council counted the funds raised, it was discovered that, despite all the public appeals, the amount collected fell far short of the target. With preparations at an advanced stage, cancelling the tour was not feasible, so the decision was made to postpone the August departure date until September, and to intensify the fund-raising campaign.

On 16 September 1888 the 'Invaders' boarded the *Wisconsin* and, after a nine-day journey, they arrived in New York to a heroes' welcome, with representatives of the Irish Societies clamouring to greet them. The tour visited several areas in New York, Boston, Philadelphia, Trenton, Newark, Patterson, Providence and Lowell. They were greeted with a tumultuous welcome in each centre and the press were generous in their coverage of the games, with hurling getting great reviews. From a social viewpoint, the tour was a success and helped establish the GAA in the US. However, influences outside their control ultimately led to the trip being considered a failure. The Invaders arrived in the US to a bitter dispute between the two rival American athletic bodies, the National American Athletic Association (NAAA) and the Amateur Athletic Union (AAU). When the GAA took a neutral position, the AAU refused to compete against them. This

A HURLEY
and sliotar from the
1888 Invasion Tour
belonging to Pat Davin.

meant that the tour no longer had the draw of the international contests between the Irish and the best American athletes. The tour lost much of its appeal and gate receipts suffered.

Attendances throughout the tour were also affected by the poor, sometimes hostile weather, which in one case resulted in the abandonment of a hurling match half-way through. Had the tour gone ahead in August, as originally planned, it is most probable that attendances (and gate receipts) would have been much higher. When Davin and the other officials sat down during the last days of the tour to examine the financial position, their worst fears were confirmed. A further £450 was needed just to meet the travel and accommodation bill. Michael Davitt advanced the party the money and all the debts were cleared.

When the party left the US on 31 October 1888, its numbers had fallen – of the 51 that had arrived, 17 (and possibly more) chose to stay on permanently.

As the aim of the tour was to raise £5,000 for the staging of the Tailteann Games in 1889, the tour must be considered a financial failure. It would be 34 years before the idea of staging the Tailteann Games was raised again.

Gaelic Sunday

On 4 August 1918, the GAA organised Gaelic Sunday – a mass show of defiance in face of the British government's attempts to force the GAA to apply for permits to play Gaelic games.

In July 1918, the British banned all public meetings in Ireland, except those for which police permission had been given. Throughout July, British military and police broke up a number of meetings, including card sessions, Irish language classes and labour and union meetings. Gaelic games were targeted – the entire GAA fixture list for Sunday 14 July 1918 was cancelled and on 28 July the police blocked the gates of Croke Park and would not allow the scheduled matches to go ahead.

On 20 July 1918 Luke O'Toole told the GAA Central Council that Dublin Castle had confirmed that no more Gaelic games could take place without a police permit. The Central Council ruled that under no circumstances whatsoever would the GAA apply for permits to play Gaelic games and, furthermore, that any GAA member taking part in a competition that had applied for, or received, a permit would be indefinitely suspended. Lastly, the GAA decided to stage a series of local games throughout Ireland at 3.00 pm on 4 August 1918.

To prepare for what quickly became known as 'Gaelic Sunday', county boards throughout Ireland held meetings at which the clubs were informed of the plans, with fixtures scheduled. By 1 August, approximately 1,500 matches had been organised, but it was unclear if the authorities would take action against any of the fixtures.

Gaelic Sunday was a huge success, with all the games played (apart from 40 games in Cork which were cancelled due to heavy rain) without interference from the military or police. The two Dublin intermediate football semi-finals were played in Croke Park, with the police remaining outside the ground. It is estimated that 54,000 people took part in Gaelic Sunday – following its success, Gaelic games were played with minimal interference from the British authorities.

Bloody Sunday (Domhnach na Fola) 1920

TICKET
for the 1920
Dublin v Tipperary
challenge game.

The most infamous event in the history of the
GAA occurred on 21 November 1920. The date is
now remembered as Bloody Sunday.

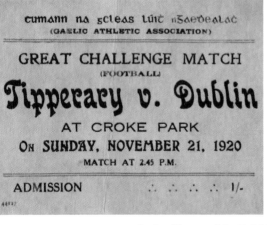

cumann na gcleas lúit ngaedealac
(GAELIC ATHLETIC ASSOCIATION)

GREAT CHALLENGE MATCH
(FOOTBALL)

Tipperary v. Dublin

AT CROKE PARK
On SUNDAY, NOVEMBER 21, 1920
MATCH AT 2.45 P.M.

ADMISSION   ∴ ∴ ∴ 1/-

Background

The War of
Independence was
raging in Ireland. On
the morning of 21
November 1920 an
assassination unit known
as 'The Squad', under the
command of Michael
Collins, mounted an
operation to take out
the backbone of the British intelligence network in
Ireland. The task was to focus on a group of British
intelligence officers known as 'The Cairo Gang', and

shootings occurred that morning, mainly around Dublin's south inner city. Following the operation, 12 agents were dead, including two members of the British Auxiliary Force. It is thought that the events that occurred later that day in Croke Park were in direct retaliation for these deaths.

Events at Croke Park

On that same day, the GAA had organised a challenge Gaelic football match between Dublin and Tipperary, two of the most successful teams of the time. The game was intended to raise funds for families of Irish political prisoners and throw-in was scheduled for 3.15 pm. Despite the concerns of GAA officials, the match began as planned, with referee Mick Sammon throwing in the ball in front of a crowd of about 10,000 spectators.

As the match started, the crowd were unaware that the British Auxiliary Forces had been given orders to advance to the area and surround Croke Park, blocking the exits, while members of the Royal Irish Constabulary (RIC) were instructed to stop and search every male attending the match as they filed out of the stadium. The teams played on inside the stadium and the crowd didn't pay much attention to an aeroplane flying low over the grounds and circling the area a couple of times before releasing a red flare from the cockpit.

Outside the grounds, an armed convoy continued to move towards Croke Park. As they did so, the uniformed men opened fire. This shooting continued as the convoy entered the pitch at the Railway End (Davin Stand area), to the shock of the spectators and players, who began to panic, causing a stampede. Rapid fire continued for about 90 seconds

as the spectators scattered around the grounds.

On the pitch, Tipperary half-back Michael (Mick) Hogan from Grangemockler crawled towards the top end of the field where he felt a sudden pain in his back. 'I'm shot,' he said. A spectator called Tom Ryan from Wexford ran towards Hogan and whispered the Act of Contrition into his ear; then he himself was hit by a bullet.

THE TIPPERARY TEAM who faced Dublin in Croke Park on Bloody Sunday.

The Aftermath

That afternoon, after 90 seconds of shooting, 13 people lay dead. Those killed included Jane Boyle, who had attended the match with her fiancée, and two children, John William Scott (14) and Jerome O'Leary (10). Michael Hogan was the only player to die that day. Over 80 people were injured and another spectator, Thomas Hogan, died later in hospital.

The year 1920 was a huge test for the GAA as the War of Independence escalated and it became impossible to organise matches. This meant that the 1920 All-Ireland senior football final was not played until 11 June 1922. Fittingly, the final was between the two counties who had been in Croke Park on Bloody Sunday – Dublin and Tipperary.

The greatest tribute to Michael Hogan came in 1925 when the GAA Central Council took the decision to name a stand in Croke Park in his honour. A plaque to commemorate those who died in Croke Park on Bloody Sunday is also displayed in the Hogan Stand.

The Names of Those who Died in Croke Park on Bloody Sunday 1920

Jane Boyle, James Burke, Daniel Carroll, Michael Feery, Michael Hogan, Thomas (Tom) Hogan, James Matthews, Patrick O'Dowd, Jerome O'Leary, William (Perry) Robinson, Tom Ryan, John William (Billy) Scott, James Teehan, Joseph Traynor.

The 1924 Tailteann Games and Rodeo

In August 1924 Croke Park staged two very different events – the 1924 Tailteann Games and Ireland's first rodeo.

In founding the GAA, one of the primary aims of Michael Cusack and Maurice Davin was the revival of the ancient Tailteann Games (An Aonach Tailteann).

The original Tailteann Games were initiated in Meath in 1896 BC as funeral games to celebrate the life of Queen Tailté, with the last games taking place in 1169 AD. The failure of the 1888 American Invasion Tour, which had been undertaken to raise funds for a Tailteann festival, meant that the idea had all but disappeared from the agenda of the GAA until 1922.

Following the Irish War of Independence (1919–21), the government of the Irish Free State began planning a modern Tailteann Games as a very public and international expression of an independent Irish nation. These amateur games were to provide an exhibition of the best in Irish sports and athleticism; the competitions were open to all people of Irish birth and to those whose parents or grandparents were Irish.

Croke Park was chosen as the main venue and the government awarded the GAA a grant of £10,000 to refurbish the stadium for the games. However, this money was given to the GAA on condition that all events held in Croke Park during the festival would be free of charge to spectators. The Irish Civil War caused the planned games to be postponed, but when it ended in May 1923, the Cosgrave Government once again pressed ahead with the planning of the Tailteann Games, now scheduled for August 1924.

The games took place predominantly in Dublin, between 2 and 18 August 1924. On the opening day, there was an industrial parade through the streets of Dublin, in which Irish manufacturing firms showcased their goods, while shops in Dublin took part in a window-dressing competition. Dublin citizens also joined in by decorating their homes and streets for the occasion. The official opening ceremony of the festival, attended by 20,000 spectators, took place later that day in Croke Park, and began with the symbolic entry to the stadium of Queen Tailté, followed by the competitors, including the popular motor-cycle convoy. Throughout the festival, there were Gaelic football, hurling, shinty, handball and athletic competitions in Croke Park, while elsewhere there were billiards games, a chess tournament and musical competitions. The biggest events in terms of spectator numbers were the motor-cycle and air-races, both of which were held in the Phoenix Park and attracted 40,000 and 20,000 spectators respectively. The festival ended with a great reception and banquet for all competitors that was held in the Central Hall of the RDS in Ballsbridge.

On the very day the Tailteann Games finished, one of the most unusual events ever held in Croke Park began. Commencing on 18 August 1924, and continuing twice-daily for seven consecutive days, Ireland's first rodeo was held in Croke Park. Newspaper advertisements described the spectacle as a 'Championship Exhibition of Cowboy Sports' and invited people to visit Croke Park to 'see just how vicious an outlaw horse can be'. Approximately 20,000 people thronged to Croke Park to see the first show, with

the Governor-General and the president of
Ireland among the guests. Throughout the
week, spectators were treated to cowboy clowns,
fancy roping displays, steer wrestling and trick
riding. The rodeo was a huge success, attracting
over 20,000 spectators each day, with special
excursion trains running to the capital from
different parts of the country each day.

**PHOTOGRAPH AND
PROGRAMME COVER**
of the rodeo that was held
in Croke Park in 1924.

1947 Polo Grounds Final

The 1947 All-Ireland senior football final.
between Cavan and Kerry was played in the
Polo Grounds, New York.

THE 1947 CAVAN TEAM with the Sam Maguire Cup.

It is the only final ever to have been played outside Ireland.

On 6 April 1947, 200 delegates at the Annual Congress considered the one remaining motion, which proposed that the GAA play the 1947 All-Ireland senior football final. in New York.

The man proposing the motion, Canon Michael Hamilton, made a speech in which he presented three key reasons why New York should host the football final. He suggested that such an event would provide a much needed stimulus to Gaelic games in the US; that, in terms of propaganda, the playing of the final in New York would be a landmark in the history of the Association; and that it would give thousands of exiled Gaels the chance to attend an All-Ireland final. Hamilton also referred to the fact that 1947 was the centenary year of the Irish famine, during which tens of thousands of Irish people emigrated to America.

THE KERRY TEAM
arriving in New York for the 1947 All-Ireland senior football final.

After Hamilton's speech, the motion was discussed with information sought on points including costs, grounds, whether this was to be taken as a precedent and would it be an inducement to emigration. Eventually the motion was passed, by a large majority, with the amendment that 'it applied to the All-Ireland Football final and for 1947 only'.

CAVAN'S MICK HIGGINS taking a shot at goal during the 1947 All-Ireland senior football final..

With the motion passed, it was now up to the GAA Central Council to decide if the staging of the final in New York was feasible and, if so, to organise it. Padraig Ó Caoimh, General Secretary of the GAA, and Tomas Kilcoyne, a member of the Central Council, visited New York on 25 April 1947 and spent three weeks investigating all aspects of the proposed final. Their feasibility report was submitted to the Central Council and studied in detail at its meeting on 23 May. Interestingly, the main bone of contention was transport to and from New York. Travelling by air in 1947 was still regarded not only as novel, but dangerous. When the vote was taken, 20 members voted for the final to go ahead in

New York, with 17 voting against it.

In many ways, deciding to hold the final in New York was the easy part; the logistics of staging the game now had to be undertaken. Ó Caoimh had too many work commitments in Ireland so Padraig McNamee travelled to New York in his place. The Polo Grounds were immediately booked for 14 September as the venue for the final. McNamee set up an office in the Woodstock Hotel and efficiently went about organising the final. Transport was arranged for the teams, with 40 to travel by plane and the remaining 25 by boat. Accommodation was booked, with the Cavan team staying in the Empire Hotel, the Kerry team in the Henry Hudson and the officials in the Hotel Woodstock.

The first party of players and officials arrived by boat on 9 September, with the remainder arriving by plane on 10 September. On 11 September, the whole party assembled at the Commodore Hotel and they were driven along Broadway escorted by a squadron of police officers. They were received at City Hall by the New York mayor, William O'Dwyer, and then transported to the Roosevelt Hotel for a gala luncheon. The teams spent the remainder of the week training.

On the day of the final, Sunday 14 September, the entire party attended High Mass at St Patrick's

Cathedral. The two teams arrived at the Polo
Grounds at 2.00 pm. At 2.40 pm the officials
and teams came on the field and met with a
tremendous reception. The teams marched into
position and stood facing the flags of the two
nations while the New York City Police Band
played 'Faith of Our Fathers' and both national
anthems. Mayor O'Dwyer started the game.
In his final report, Ó Caoimh called it a 'game
that will live forever in the memory of those
privileged to witness it'. The final result was
Cavan 2-11, Kerry 2-07.

That night a banquet was held in the
Commodore Hotel, with 1,500 people
attending. The following week, on 22
September, an evening match between a Cavan–
Kerry selection and a New York selection was
played for the benefit of the New York GAA.
The entire party sailed home on 24 September,
arriving in Dún Laoghaire on 3 October.

THE HOMECOMING PARADE
for the 1947
Cavan team.

DOUGLAS HYDE, who, as president of Ireland, was removed as a patron of the GAA for attending a soccer game.

Ban on Foreign Games and the Opening Up of Croke Park

The so-called GAA 'ban on foreign games' had a long and controversial history; first introduced in 1885 to stifle competition from the rival Irish Amateur Athletic Association (IAAA), the ban was relaxed, repealed and then reintroduced in 1901, albeit in voluntary form.

In 1902 the ban was made compulsory, with the added introduction of vigilance committees, whose role was to attend 'foreign games', mainly soccer and rugby, and 'spy' on GAA members who were in breach of the ban. This version of the 'ban' remained in place until its removal in 1971.

The ban, however, was not universally appreciated by GAA members and caused a few controversies. In 1911 the London County Board voted to repeal the ban, but the London chairman, Liam MacCarthy, refused to travel to Dublin to bring this motion to the 1911 Annual Convention, as he himself was against any relaxation of the rule.

The biggest controversy surrounding the ban erupted in 1938 when the GAA removed Douglas Hyde, president of Ireland, as a patron of the GAA, for attending an international soccer match.

The fall-out that resulted from this decision was spectacular, with the media ridiculing the GAA's decision. However, the controversial decision was effectively ratified by the GAA at their 1939 Annual Congress, when 120 members voted against the reinstatement of Hyde, with only 11 voting in favour.

The beginning of the end for the ban came in 1959, when the Dublin Civil Service GAA Club, led by its chairman, Tom Woulfe, started a decade-long campaign to have the ban removed. Woulfe relentlessly attacked the ban and its supporters. Although Woulfe's efforts were frustrated in 1962, 1965 and 1968 (the ban could only be discussed at Congress every three years), by 1971 a total of 30 counties had called for the removal of the ban, with only Sligo and Antrim calling for its retention. By the time of the 1971 Annual Congress, held on Easter Sunday, 11 April 1971, the repeal of the ban was a foregone conclusion.

Somewhat related to the ban on foreign games was Rule 42, which prohibited field games other than Gaelic games being played in GAA grounds.

Games that were a direct threat to the GAA, in particular soccer and rugby, were not allowed. In the early to mid-2000s, calls were made from within and outside the GAA to open up Croke Park to both soccer and rugby, particularly when plans were announced to redevelop the Lansdowne Road stadium.

In 2005 the rule was finally modified to allow the playing of soccer and rugby in Croke

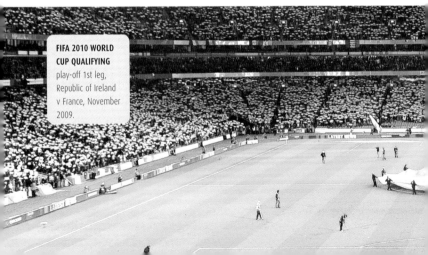

FIFA 2010 WORLD CUP QUALIFYING play-off 1st leg, Republic of Ireland v France, November 2009.

Park while Lansdowne Road was being redeveloped. Following negotiations with the Irish Rugby Football Union (IRFU) and the Football Association of Ireland (FAI), history was made on 11 February 2007 when the first rugby game (Ireland v France) was played in Croke Park, with the first soccer match (Ireland v Wales) taking place on 24 March 2007. In between these two games, Croke Park staged the Ireland v England rugby international, which is seen as one of the most symbolic moments in the history of sport in Ireland.

Playing Rule Changes 1884–2015

When the GAA was formed in 1884, one of the first tasks undertaken by Michael Cusack and Maurice Davin was to draft rules for hurling and Gaelic football – 10 rules for football and 12 for hurling were agreed upon.

A GAELIC FOOTBALL MATCH in progress in 1903, with the 'old style' points posts visible.

These two sets of rules were subsequently adopted at the second meeting of the GAA, held in Cork in December 1884, and published in the *United Ireland* newspaper in February 1885. Over the next few years, as arguments arose, these rules were added to, in an effort to regulate the games properly.

Some of the major rule changes that have taken place include the following innovations.

Initially, there were only soccer-style goal posts, with points posts introduced in 1886. Points posts were placed at either side of the goal posts; these points posts were abolished in 1910 in favour of today's H-shaped posts.

In the very early games, forfeit points were awarded in place of today's 45 and 65 frees: when a team played the ball over its own end line (but outside of the goal and points posts), the opposing team was awarded a 'forfeit' point, with five forfeit points equal to one goal. Forfeit points were abolished in 1886 and replaced with today's free kick/puck.

In 1884, football and hurling teams were 21 a side; this was reduced to 17 a side in 1896, and in 1913 the teams were further reduced to 15 a side, which is the team size today.

MATCH PROGRAMME cover for the 1913 All-Ireland senior football final.

While goals initially outweighed any number of points, with points taken into consideration only when the two teams scored an equal number of goals, a goal was made equal to five points from 1892 and to three points in 1896.

The original time of play for Gaelic football matches was one hour, while hurling games lasted 80 minutes. In 1886 this was changed so that the

games for both codes lasted one hour. In 1970 the playing time was increased to 80 minutes for senior championship games, but in 1975 this was reduced to 70 minutes.

In 1999, yellow and red cards were introduced. These caused some controversy on their first day when six red cards and 14 yellow cards were flashed during the Carlow v Westmeath Leinster football championship game. An additional black card, for certain cynical fouls, was introduced for football games in January 2014.

REFEREE NIALL BARRETT
sends off Carlow's Brian Farrell in 1999.

GAA Anniversaries: 1934, 1959, 1984 and 2009

On Easter Sunday, 1 April 1934, the GAA celebrated its Golden Jubilee by holding its Annual Congress in Thurles, birthplace of the Association.

In the morning, GAA officials received and read numerous messages of support from throughout Ireland at the Confraternity Hall, before attending High Mass at Thurles Cathedral. Afterwards, GAA representatives led a large public procession through Thurles, around the Croke Memorial in the town to Hayes Hotel, where a commemorative plaque was unveiled. Over 200 people then attended lunch in Hayes Hotel, including three members of the victorious Tipperary hurling team from the first All-Ireland championship and Michael Cusack's son John. At the Annual Congress itself, held in the Confraternity Hall, Tom Semple's suggestion that the 1934 All-Ireland hurling final be played in Thurles was ruled out of order, with the compromise motion to play an eight-team hurling competition in Thurles passed instead.

For their 75th anniversary, the GAA officially opened the new Hogan Stand at Croke Park on 7 June 1959. The opening of this double-decker stand was attended by 23,300 people, including 900 holders of All-Ireland medals and included a

WORKERS
hoist seats into the newly built Hogan Stand in 1959.

MATCH PROGRAMME COVER for the 1984 All-Ireland hurling final in Thurles.

CLÁR OIFIGIÚIL

Cluichí Ceannais Iomána na hÉireann

CLG

Stáid Semple,
Durlas
2 Meán Fomhair 1984

CORCAIGH v UIBH FHAILÍ
Pascal Long (Cill Chainnigh) 3.30 i.n.

Cill Chainnigh v Luimneach
Frank Murphy (Corcaigh) 1.30 i.n.

100

Bliain Comóradh An Chéid

Luach £1

blessing by Monsignor O'Reilly and speeches from both the president of the GAA, Dr J. J. Stuart, and the president of Ireland, Dr Seán T. O'Kelly. A pageant, entitled *The Pageant of the Flag*, which depicted outstanding events in Ireland's history from 1798 until 1959, was performed on the pitch, then the ceremonies concluded with the playing of the Railway Cup hurling final between Munster (7-11) and Connacht (2-06).

Some 50 years after rejecting Tom Semple's suggestion, the GAA agreed to hold the All-Ireland hurling final in Semple Stadium, Thurles, as part of the Association's centenary celebrations in 1984. This was the first time that an All-Ireland hurling final had been held outside Dublin since 1937. While the game itself, in which Cork beat Offaly by 3-16 to 1-12, was described by one national newspaper as a 'one-sided drab affair', Raymond Smith wrote in the *Irish Independent* that the 'day itself, the pageantry, the colour, and the wonderful pre-match atmosphere in Liberty Square will remain etched in the memories of all those privileged to be in the cradle of the G.A.A. yesterday.'

Apart from the hurling final, the GAA also ran All-Ireland centenary hurling and football competitions, won by Cork and Meath respectively, while, in conjunction with the *Sunday Independent*, a Team of the Century was chosen for both hurling and football. Clubs were also encouraged to produce a written history, and an abundance of fine books was published as a result of this.

In 2009 the GAA celebrated its 125th anniversary. The festivities started with a fireworks extravaganza at the national football league match between Dublin and Tyrone on 31 January. On St Patrick's Day, some of the top GAA players acted as grand marshalls in

the Dublin parade. On 10 May, GAA clubs throughout the world celebrated the anniversary by organising games and cultural events as part of the year's Lá na gClub. In July, President Mary McAleese hosted a garden party at Áras an Uachtaráin, with four nominated guests from every county invited – one county officer, one player and two volunteers. Guests at this party were entertained by the Artane Band. In September, the hurling and football finals in Croke Park were marked by colour and pageantry. As the year drew to a close, *The GAA: A People's History* was published, while in November the Central Bank launched a limited edition €15 coin, decorated with the GAA 125 logo and a hurler.

FIREWORKS
at Croke Park mark the GAA's 125th anniversary celebrations.

Stars of Camogie and Ladies Gaelic Football

Kathleen Mills (Dublin)

Dublin's Kathleen 'Kay' Mills is one of the three most decorated players in the history of Gaelic games. She won an amazing 15 All-Ireland medals during her 20-year inter-county career. She retired from the playing field in 1941 at the age of 38. In recognition of her achievements, each year the junior All-Ireland winning captain receives a trophy bearing her name. Kathleen's impressive medal collection is on display in the GAA Museum.

Briege Corkery (Cork)

In 2015 a convincing display by the Cork ladies footballers to claim their 10th senior All-Ireland title in 11 years

KATHLEEN MILLS
lifting one of her trophies.

meant that dual star Briege Corkery was able to equal Kathleen Mills's impressive and unbeaten haul of 15 All-Ireland medals. Briege's medal collection includes six All-Ireland camogie medals (these were won in 2005, 2006, 2008, 2014 and 2015), and nine ladies football titles (these were won in 2005, 2006, 2007, 2009, 2011, 2012, 2013, 2014 and 2015).

Rena Buckley (Cork)

Another Cork dual star to have won an amazing 15 All-Ireland medals across both codes is Rena Buckley from the Inniscarra club. Rena is also an All-Star in both codes.

27 SEPTEMBER 2015
Cork players Briege Corkery and Rena Buckley, who have both won 16 All-Ireland senior ladies football medals, are among the most decorated women in the GAA.

Iconic Footballers

Tommy Murphy (Laois)

A midfielder for Laois from 1937 to 1953, Tommy won three Leinster medals. He was honoured as part of the Football Team of the Millennium. He was the only player named on the team who had not won an All-Ireland medal.

In 2004 a new football competition was introduced – the Tommy Murphy Cup. Teams who left the football championship in the early stages joined the Tommy Murphy Cup competition. However, it was short-lived competition and ended in 2008.

THE CAVAN FOOTBALL TEAM that won the 1947 All-Ireland football final in New York.

John Joe O'Reilly (Cavan)

John Joseph O'Reilly was the inspirational captain during Cavan's glory years of the 1940s. He is regarded as a footballing legend and is immortalised in the song 'The Gallant John Joe'.

He led his county to victory in 1947 and 1948 –
he is one of only seven men who have had the honour
of being presented with the Sam Maguire twice as
captain. John Joe passed away at a young age. The great
era of Cavan football lives on in his name.

Seán Flanagan (Mayo)

Captain of the All-Ireland-winning Mayo sides of
1950 and 1951, Seán's display in the 1950 final is
considered one of the greatest ever by a defender in a
football final. Seán also won five Connacht
titles and two national football league titles (1949
and 1954). While still a footballer, he began a career
in politics, representing Fianna Fáil in East Mayo. He
also served in the European Parliament in the 1980s.

Seán Purcell (Galway)

Known as 'the master', he won a staggering 10 senior
county championships with his club, Tuam Stars.
He won an All-Ireland medal with Galway in 1956,

SEÁN FLANAGAN.

MICK O'CONNELL
in action during the
1968 All-Ireland
senior football final.

where his dazzling on-field partnership with Frank
Stockwell earned them the title 'the terrible twins'.
He also won a national football league title and six
Connacht titles with Galway, and three Railway Cups
with Connacht (1951, 1957 and 1958).

Mick O'Connell (Kerry)

Mick O'Connell, from Valentia Island, made his debut
on the Kerry senior football team in 1956. His career
spanned more than three decades. He won eight
Munster senior titles in a row, from 1958 to 1965.
He also won four All-Irelands (1959, 1962, 1969 and
1970). He retired from inter-county football in 1973.

Seán O'Neill (Down)

Seán was a member of the Down team that won the 1960 All-Ireland senior football final. This was the first time Sam Maguire went over the border. Down retained the cup in 1961 – the final had the highest attendance ever recorded at a match in Croke Park, with 90,556 supporters in the stands.

Seán won a third All-Ireland in 1968, the year in which he was awarded the Footballer of the Year award. He won eight Ulster championships and three national football leagues with Down.

When his playing days were over, Seán became involved in management with Queen's University, Belfast, which won the Sigerson cup in 1982, 1984 and 1985.

SEÁN O'NEILL in action during the 1960 All-Ireland senior football final..

Dermot Earley Snr (Roscommon)

A leading figure in Connacht and Roscommon football, Dermot won five Connacht senior medals with Roscommon, in 1972, 1977, 1978, 1979 and

DERMOT EARLEY
in action for
Roscommon
in 1985.

1980. He also won a national football league medal, an All-Ireland under-21 title and two Railway Cups during his playing career. He was the recipient of two All-Star awards.

After retiring as a player he managed the Kildare and Roscommon county teams.

Dermot also achieved great success in his military career, reaching the rank of Chief-of-Staff of the Irish Defence Forces.

Jimmy Keaveney (Dublin)

Jimmy was a member of the famous Dublin football team of the 1970s. He had a successful 14-year career with Dublin, winning three All-Ireland medals and six Leinster championships and national football leagues. Individually, Keaveney won many accolades – three All-Star awards and back-to-back Footballer of the Year awards in 1976 and 1977.

Jimmy was a key figure in his club, St Vincent's. During his playing career he won 10 Dublin

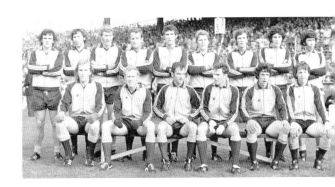

THE 1977 DUBLIN TEAM
Jimmy Keaveney is standing in the back row, fourth from left.

senior county championships, and a coveted All-Ireland club championship in 1976. He was inducted into the GAA Hall of Fame in 2015.

Pat Spillane (Kerry)

Pat Spillane is considered to be one of the greatest Gaelic footballers of his generation. He made his senior inter-county debut in 1974, and over a 17-year inter-county career with Kerry, he won eight All-Ireland medals and was part of the famous Kerry four-in-a-row team. Other honours include four national football league medals, four Railway Cup medals and nine All-Star awards, more than any other player in Gaelic football.

Spillane's career also included four appearances with Ireland in the International Rules series in 1986 and 1987.

Spillane was presented with the coveted Footballer of the Year award in 1978 and 1984. His second win was all the more remarkable, given that he had fought his way back from a career-threatening injury.

Spillane was also chosen for the left wing-forward position on the Football Team of the Millennium in 1999.

Following his retirement from Gaelic football, Spillane went on to develop a career in the media. Since 1992, he has been part of *The Sunday Game* line-up as a commentator and studio analyst.

Maurice Fitzgerald (Kerry)

The Cahirciveen and St Mary's clubman made his senior championship debut against Waterford in 1988. In the same year, he won a coveted Sigerson Cup medal with UCC.

Maurice Fitzgerald is probably best remembered for his performance in the 1997 All-Ireland final against Mayo, and his legendary side-line point against Dublin in an All-Ireland quarter-final in Thurles back in 2001. This latter achievement was later listed as one of the Top 20 GAA Moments.

In 1997 Kerry defeated Ulster champions Cavan in the All-Ireland semi-final to qualify for their first All-Ireland final in 11 years. They defeated Mayo, with

Fitzgerald the star player for Kerry, scoring nine points during the game. His performances throughout the championship and in the so-called 'Maurice Fitzgerald final' earned him a third All-Star award; he was also named All-Star Footballer of the Year and Texaco Footballer of the Year.

During his senior inter-county career, Maurice Fitzgerald won two All-Ireland titles, six Munster championships, a national football league and three All-Star awards.

Peter Canavan (Tyrone)

He is called 'Peter the Great' in his native Tyrone, and was the first Tyrone captain to lift the Sam Maguire when they beat Kerry in the All-Ireland final in 2003. Peter went on to another All-Ireland victory with Tyrone in 2005. He also has two national football leagues and five Ulster championship medals.

During his 16 years playing senior football for Tyrone, he was renowned for his score-taking ability.

MAURICE FITZGERALD
during a game.

PETER CANAVAN
celebrates during
the 2005 All-Ireland
senior football final..

Peter holds the mantle of the most awards for an
Ulster footballer, with six All-Stars to his name.

At club level, Canavan also enjoyed success with
Errigal Ciarán GAC, winning six Tyrone senior
club medals as well as two Ulster club titles. He also
managed them in 2009 when they won the Tyrone
All County League. He managed the Fermanagh
footballers from 2011 to 2013.

Colm 'the Gooch' Cooper (Kerry)

Cooper is considered to be one of the most gifted
and skilful players of the current generation of
footballers. He began his inter-county career with
the Kerry senior team in 2002 and has enjoyed an
illustrious career. He has won five senior All-Ireland
titles with Kerry and seven Munster titles. He has also
won eight All-Star awards during his career. Colm has
also enjoyed success with his club, Dr Crokes from
Killarney, winning four Munster club championships.

COLM COOPER.

Iconic Hurlers

Mick Mackey (Limerick)

Limerick's Mick Mackey is unquestionably one of the all-time hurling greats. In the late 1930s the Ahane club man played a key role in a side that dominated the scene and won three All-Ireland senior hurling titles as well as five Munster championship titles and five national hurling league medals. During his career with the Limerick senior team, Mackey made 42 championship appearances, usually at centre-forward. He was named in this position on the Hurling Team of the Century in 1984 and on the Hurling Team of the Millennium in 2000.

Christy Ring (Cork)

Cork's Christy Ring reigns supreme as the undisputed kingpin of hurling. His career spanned two decades and his prowess on the pitch was a sight to behold. During his memorable time in the Cork jersey, he won eight All-Ireland senior medals and was also a star of the Railway Cup competition, where he made

CHRISTY RING
in action.

44 appearances for Munster and clocked up 18 winners' medals. Sadly, Ring died prematurely aged 58 in 1979. His medal collection is on display in the GAA Museum in Croke Park.

Nickey Rackard (Wexford)

Nickey Rackard's memory is so important to the people of Wexford that a statue of him is displayed in Wexford town. The man from Killane played for the county during a golden age of hurling in the southeast. He won two All-Ireland medals, four Leinster titles and one national hurling league medal wearing the purple and gold. Rackard remains in the list of the top 10 highest hurling championship scorers of all time, clocking up an amazing 59 goals and 96 points during 36 appearances for Wexford. Rackard was also a keen Gaelic footballer and won one Leinster medal in this code. He was selected for full-forward position on the Hurling Team of the Century.

Jimmy Doyle (Tipperary)

With six All-Ireland senior hurling titles, seven national hurling league medals and nine Munster senior hurling titles under his belt, Jimmy Doyle of Tipperary certainly had an impressive playing career. He also had the honour of captaining Tipperary to All-Ireland glory

and he lifted the Liam MacCarthy as team captain in Croke Park in both 1962 and 1965. With his club, Thurles-Sarsfield's, Doyle claimed 10 county championship medals in hurling and also represented Munster in the Railway Cup for 12 years, winning eight medals along the way. He was named Hurler of the Year in 1965 and was selected for left-corner forward on the Hurling Team of the Millennium.

Joe Cooney (Galway)

Joe played centre-forward on the Galway inter-county team.

During his playing career, he enjoyed great success with Galway. He won two All-Ireland senior medals when Galway won back-to-back titles in 1987 and 1988. His brother Jimmy won an All-Ireland with Galway in 1980, on a team that also included the Connolly brothers – Joe, John and Michael. Joe was also part of four Galway teams that were runners-up in All-Ireland finals.

In 1987 he was named Hurler of the Year. He won a total of five All-Star awards in six seasons.

Joe is a member of the Sarsfield GAA club in Galway, winning back-to back All-Ireland club titles in 1993 and 1994.

In 2009 he was listed in an *Irish Independent* poll as one of the top hurlers of 125 years of the GAA.

Nicky English (Tipperary)

Nicky English of the Lattin-Cullen club has achieved All-Ireland success with his native

JOE COONEY.

Tipperary as a manager and player. Known for his dominance leading the forward line, English won two All-Irelands, five Munster championships and two national hurling league medals with the Tipperary senior hurlers. In 1989 he claimed his sixth All-Star and was named Hurler of the Year. As a manager, English guided Tipperary to two national hurling league titles as well as an All-Ireland senior hurling title in 2001. He has worked as a hurling co-commentator with Irish television station TV3.

NICKY ENGLISH
playing for Tipperary.

D. J. Carey (Kilkenny)

In a county that churns out star hurlers, Denis Joseph 'D. J.' Carey stands out as exceptional. With five All-Ireland senior medals, 10 Leinster senior titles, four national hurling league medals, two Railway Cup titles and an impressive nine All-Star awards, he is one of Ireland's most successful sports stars and is known

D. J. CAREY
playing for Kilkenny.

for his amazing scoring ability and eye for goal. His skilful performances for Kilkenny saw him named Hurler of the Year in 1993 and 2000. He also had a successful handball career and won a number of All-Ireland and world titles.

BRIAN WHELAHAN
playing for Offaly
in 2000.

Brian Whelahan (Offaly)

As well as being an outstanding player at senior county level, Brian Whelahan also had success at college and club levels. He helped his club, Birr, to 12 county titles, seven Leinster club titles and four All-Ireland titles, and also claimed two All-Ireland minor hurling medals with Offaly. In 1994 Brian won his first All-Ireland senior hurling medal and was named Hurler of the Year. In 1998 he repeated the feat, putting in an impressive performance in the final against Kilkenny and, despite suffering from flu, scoring 1-6 to clinch the title. Whelahan's legendary status was confirmed when he was selected at left wing-back on the Hurling Team of the Millennium, the only player still playing at the time of selection.

Henry Shefflin (Kilkenny)

Henry Shefflin has secured his place in GAA history as one of hurling's greatest ever players. 'King' Henry, as he is referred to affectionately, made 71 championship appearances and holds the record as the all-time top scorer in the All-Ireland senior hurling championship, with 27 goals and 484 points. Shefflin was part of a dominant Kilkenny side that won 10 All-Irelands between 2000 and 2014 and he has made an appearance in 15 All-Ireland finals (including two replays). He was named Hurler of the Year three times and has won 11 All-Star awards. With Ballyhale Shamrocks, Shefflin won three All-Ireland club medals.

HENRY SHEFFLIN
with the Liam MacCarthy Cup, 2014.

Football Managers: Joe Kernan

The Crossmaglen Rangers club in south Armagh is synonymous with provincial and All-Ireland success.

JOE KERNAN celebrates after Crossmaglen Rangers win the 1999 All-Ireland Senior Club Football title.

Since 1997, the club has reached the All-Ireland decider on 10 occasions, winning six times. At the centre of this success is the Kernan family.

Joe Kernan managed Crossmaglen Rangers between 1993 and 2000 and steered the club to three All-Ireland Club titles in four years. Kernan's four sons – Paul, Aaron, Stephen and Tony – have won 11 All-Ireland club medals between them, and all four have played with the Armagh county team. These medals are on display in the GAA Museum at Croke Park.

Joe also managed the Armagh senior footballers from 2002 until 2007. In 2002 Armagh won their first and only All-Ireland title. He also managed the Galway footballers from 2009 to 2010. In 2015 Joe managed the Ireland International Rules team that won the Cormac McAnallen cup.

Joe played for Armagh from 1971 until 1987. In 1977 he scored two goals in the All-Ireland final against Dublin, although Armagh lost the game. He won an All-Star award in 1977.

ARMAGH CAPTAIN
Kieran McGeeney lifts the Sam Maguire in front of the Armagh fans, 22 September 2002.

Football Managers: Kevin Heffernan

TEAM OF THE MILLENNIUM commemorative stamp featuring Kevin Heffernan.

Kevin Heffernan, or 'Heffo', as he was affectionately known, is regarded as one of the greatest Gaelic footballers of all time.

Born in Dublin in 1929, Heffernan was brought up in Marino and went on to enjoy a lifelong connection with the St Vincent's Club. He attended the local Scoil Mhuire and St Joseph's CBS in Fairview, where he was part of the team that won the 1945 Leinster colleges hurling title. He excelled at both codes at minor level for Dublin, winning a Leinster title in football in 1946 and one in hurling in 1947.

As a senior player, Heffernan was part of the Dublin side that won the Leinster title in 1955, before being beaten by Kerry in the All-Ireland final, a rivalry that would later define his career as a manager. His best year as a player came in 1958 when he captained Dublin to the league and All-Ireland double. He subsequently won Leinster titles in 1959 and 1962 before retiring from playing at inter-county level. Heffernan's club career is one of the most decorated in the history of the game. He won 21 Dublin senior titles in total – 15 in football and six in hurling. Included in the football wins was a sequence of seven-in-a-row from 1949 to 1955 and a sequence of six-in-a row from 1957 to 1962. His six Dublin hurling titles came between 1953 and 1962, all in years when St Vincent's also won the football title.

Heffernan's career as Dublin manager began in late 1973, and in 1974 he guided the team to their first Leinster and All-Ireland titles in a decade. This achievement won him the 1974 Footballer of the Year award, the only non-player to win it. Dublin lost the 1975 All-Ireland final to a young Kerry side, but Heffernan and Dublin had their revenge in 1976 with a comprehensive seven-point win over Kerry in the All-Ireland final. Heffernan stood down from the post following the victory, but returned in 1978. Dublin claimed their sixth successive Leinster title that year, but Kerry again stood in their way in the final, winning this time by

KEVIN HEFFERNAN
as the Dublin
manager.

17 points as they began their four-in-a-row run of title victories. After rebuilding the side in the early 1980s, Heffernan claimed a third All-Ireland title in 1983, when the 12 men of Dublin beat the 14 men from Galway after four players were sent off in an ill-tempered final.

Heffernan was named on both the Football Team of the Century and the Team of the Millennium. He later managed Ireland to victory over Australia in the International Rules Series in 1986 and continued his coaching at St Vincent's and as a consultant to the Dublin minor team in 2007. Heffernan passed away in January 2013; in a fitting tribute to his career, both Dublin and St Vincent's won their respective All-Ireland football and Dublin championship titles that year.

Football Managers: Mick O'Dwyer

Mick O'Dwyer, a successful Gaelic football player for Kerry, is best known as one of the greatest football managers in the history of the GAA.

Having managed the iconic Kerry team in the latter half of the 1970s, O'Dwyer also managed Kildare, Wicklow, Laois and Clare.

Born in 1936, O'Dwyer played football with his local club, Waterville. At minor level, O'Dwyer won a Munster medal in 1954, but he was not included on the team that subsequently lost to Dublin in the All-Ireland minor final. O'Dwyer's move to senior level was a natural progression – he first lined out for the senior team in 1957 and won his first provincial medal the following year. In 1959 Kerry defeated Galway in the All-Ireland senior football final, giving O'Dwyer his first of three All-Ireland medals as a player. Having won another All-Ireland in 1962,

MICK O'DWYER as the Kerry manager, 1984.

disaster struck O'Dwyer in 1966 when he broke both his legs playing football; despite retiring from the game O'Dwyer returned in 1968 and won his third All-Ireland medal in 1969. In 1974, he retired as a Kerry football player.

Already in charge of the Kerry under-21 team, O'Dwyer became the manager of the senior team in 1975. He immediately replaced some of the older players with those he knew from the under-21 team. Between 1975 and his retirement in 1989, the Kerry senior team contested 10 All-Ireland finals, winning eight of them. During this time, Kerry achieved their first four-in-a-row (1978–81) since the same feat was achieved in 1929 to1932, with a famous (yet to be achieved) five-in-a-row thwarted by Seamus Darby's goal in 1982.

Having initially agreed to manage the Dublin footballers, O'Dwyer changed his mind and returned to the inter-county scene as manager of the Kildare team in 1991. Beaten by Louth in 1991 and then by Dublin in 1992 and 1993, O'Dwyer left Kildare in 1994 and returned to coach his club, Waterville. Kildare came calling again in 1997 and O'Dwyer started his second stint as their manager. This time success came in the form of two Leinster titles (1998 and 2000) and a first All-Ireland final appearance for the Lilywhites since

1935. When Kildare were knocked out of the championship in 2002, O'Dwyer decided it was time for him to leave the post.

O'Dwyer became manager of the Laois senior team at the end of 2002 and guided the team to the Leinster title in 2003. This was the first time Laois had won a Leinster title since 1946 and O'Dwyer guided the team to two more Leinster final appearances in 2004 and 2005. O'Dwyer announced that 2006 would be his last year with Laois; on 26 September that year O'Dwyer stepped down as Laois manager, only to be appointed as the Wicklow manager two weeks later. As Wicklow manager, he had a positive impact – Wicklow won the 2008 Tommy Murphy Cup, beating Antrim in the final at Croke Park. 2009 marked an incredible year for both Wicklow and O'Dwyer: Wicklow played six championship games

MICK O'DWYER
as the Wicklow manager, 2011.

MICK O'DWYER
as the Kildare
manager, 2000.

and won a championship game in Croke Park for
the first time; when the team defeated Fermanagh in
July, it marked a personal milestone for O'Dwyer –
he had now defeated every other playing county
as a manager. However, two years later, in July
2011, O'Dwyer announced the end of his tenure
with Wicklow. He managed Clare for the 2013
championship and he retired in January 2014,
bringing to an end one of the most illustrious
careers in GAA history.

MICK O'DWYER
as the Laois
manager, 2003.

Football Managers: Mickey Harte

He has become a legend in his native county Tyrone.

Mickey took over as senior inter-county manager in
2002 following successful stints as minor and under-21
Tyrone manager, winning the All-Ireland in 1998
and 2000 respectively. He was the first inter-county
manager to bring the Sam Maguire Cup to the O'Neill
county when they beat neighbours Armagh in the first
all-Ulster All-Ireland senior football final in 2003.

MICKEY HARTE.

Tyrone went on to win two further All-Irelands with the Tyrone senior team in 2005 and 2008, on both occasions beating Kerry in the final. In 2008 they took the long road to the final: they had to come through the qualifier system, having been beaten in the first Ulster round by Down after a replay. The All-Ireland final in 2008 was their eighth match of the championship.

In addition to his All-Ireland successes, Mickey has also won four Ulster championships with Tyrone and a national football league in 2003.

The Tyrone teams under Mickey Harte have been advocates of a defensive system of play and Mickey is considered a master tactician of the game. Many teams have now looked to Tyrone to adopt some elements of their game to include in their own game strategy.

A member of Errigal Ciaran GAA club, Mickey also managed their senior football team and brought them success, notably with wins in the Tyrone senior county championship and the Ulster senior football championship in 2002.

MICKEY HARTE
lifts the Sam Maguire Cup in 2008.

Football Managers: Páidí Ó Sé

Páidí was born in 1955 in Ceann Trá, in the heart of the Kerry Gaeltacht.

A native Irish speaker, he attended Dingle CBS, St Brendan's College in Killarney and St Michael's College in Listowel.

As a player, Páidí was awarded five All-Stars and won eight All-Ireland senior football medals with the Kingdom. He was captain of the All-Ireland winning team in 1985. His other playing

WESTMEATH win their first Leinster football title in 2004 under the management of Paidí Ó Sé.

credits include 11 Munster championships, four national football leagues, two county senior championships, one county junior championship, three All-Ireland under-21 championships, three Munster under-21 championships and four Railway Cups, as well as medals at colleges level.

Ó Sé also had success at inter-county level as a manager, winning two All-Ireland titles as the Kerry boss in 1997 and 2000. His time in charge also saw Kerry win six Munster titles and a national football league. After his stint with his native Kerry, Ó Sé was appointed manager of Westmeath. In his first season in charge, he led the team to their first ever Leinster senior football championship title in 2004. In 2007 Ó Sé also spent some time in charge of the Clare footballers.

Sadly, Páidí died unexpectedly in December 2012 at the age of 57. A bronze statue in memory of the Kerry legend was unveiled at his famous pub near Ventry in West Kerry in May 2015. The statue, by sculptor Séamus Connolly, shows the man himself wearing the No.5 jersey and holding a football. A bust of Páidí by the same Clare sculptor is on display in the GAA Museum at Croke Park. Páidí's nephews Feargal, Darragh, Tomás and Marc have all played for Kerry.

Football Managers: Seán Boylan

The Meath hurler and herbalist became the longest serving inter-county manager.

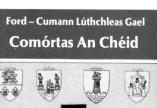

In 1983 Meath football was at a low, and the masseuse from the Meath hurling team, who had no experience or background in managing football teams, was appointed to manage the team. Over the next 23 years, Seán Boylan achieved success on the field with two different teams.

When Boylan took over the reins, Meath had not won any silverware since the 1970 Leinster championship. Within a year Meath had beaten Monaghan in the 1984 Centenary Cup final – a special competition held to celebrate the centenary of the foundation of the GAA. This win raised morale in the county and positivity grew.

In 1986 the big breakthrough came when Meath won the Leinster football championship, beating Dublin 0-9 to 0-7.

In 1987 Meath won the All-Ireland football title for the first time in 20 years. They played Cork in the final, the first of four All-Ireland finals the two counties would play against each other over the next four years, as the 1988 final was drawn, requiring a replay.

Seán Boylan's teams were synonymous with intensive play and strong defences. The training regime was also somewhat unorthodox – they were known to run up and down the Hill of Tara and wear wetsuits in the swimming pool in Gormanston College to build muscle strength.

THE 1987 Meath team.

SEÁN BOYLAN
lifts the Sam Maguire
Cup in 1999.

After winning two All-Irelands back to back in 1987 and 1988, the team members gradually retired over the next six years. Seán set about building a new team, and in 1996 Meath reached the All-Ireland finals again with a young team. Meath won the 1996 All-Ireland, beating Mayo in a replay, and in 1999 after beating Cork.

After winning the Leinster title that year, Meath went on to reach another All-Ireland final in 2001, but were beaten and outclassed by Galway. Seán Boylan managed Meath for a further four years, retiring in 2005. In recognition of his services and contribution to Meath, he was made a Freeman of Meath in 2006, the first and only person to receive this honour.

Replays

The Seán Boylan era is synonymous with replays. During his tenure as manager, Meath were drawn in two All-Ireland finals – against Cork in 1988 and against Mayo in 1996. After beating Cork in the 1988 replay, Meath won back-to-back All-Ireland titles.

The 1996 final against Mayo went to a replay when a freak last-minute point by Colm Coyle drew the game. The final replay was infamous due to a brawl that broke out minutes into the game. Meath went on to win the game and the All-Ireland by one point.

Meath and Leinster rivals Kildare were involved in three semi-final matches in the Leinster football championship. Kildare were managed by Kerry legend Mick O'Dwyer. After the first game was a draw, the teams were still tied after extra time in the replay. Meath won the second replay.

The most famous replays Boylan was involved in were the 1991 Leinster championship first-round matches against Dublin. In all there were four matches – with Meath emerging as winners in the last game.

International Rules

Boylan was selected as manager for the International Rules team in 2006. The games were played in Pearse Stadium Galway and Croke Park. They were fractious games and Boylan had concerns over the spirit in which the games were played. Australia won the 2006 series. There was a break in 2007 and when the series resumed in 2008 Boylan remained as manager, travelling to Australia for the series. Ireland won and brought the Cormac McAnallen trophy home.

Football Managers: Eamonn Ryan

Before Eamonn Ryan took over as manager of the Cork ladies football team in 2003, the county had never won a senior title – league, provincial or All-Ireland. This all changed under Ryan, however, and by 2015 the county had won an astonishing 10 All-Ireland titles (out of a possible 11), winning 27 trophies (out of a possible 33) during this period.

CORK MANAGER
Eamonn Ryan after the 2015 All-Ireland senior ladies football final, when Cork won their 10th championship title.

Ryan, a primary school teacher by profession, played football with the Glenville team in his youth and, while he never made the Cork underage teams, he debuted with the senior team in 1962, going on to play in both Munster and All-Ireland finals. As a manager, Ryan coached the Cork men's senior team to Munster success in 1983, while later guiding the Cork men's minor team to All-Ireland victory in 1991 and 1993. He also coached the Na Piarsaigh hurling team that won the 1990 and 1995 county titles. It was with the Cork ladies football team, however, that he had most success, and he is rightly regarded as one of the most successful managers in GAA history.

Hurling Managers: Brian Cody

The first name to spring to mind of all the hurling managers in all the clubs and counties across Ireland and beyond since time began is that of Brian Cody!

The unstoppable Kilkenny boss began his senior county managerial career in November 1998 and since then has gone on to lead the team to 11 All-Ireland senior hurling championship victories in 2000, 2002, 2003, 2006, 2007, 2008, 2009, 2011, 2012, 2014 and 2015. Under his stewardship, the Cats have also clocked up eight national hurling league titles and won an incredible 14 Leinster senior hurling championships.

JOHN HORGAN (Cork) in action against Brian Cody (Kilkenny) during the 1978 All-Ireland senior hurling final.

Throughout his time at the helm, Cody has guided the career of hurling superstars such as D. J.

KILKENNY MANAGER

Brian Cody during the 2015 All-Ireland senior hurling final.

Carey, Henry Shefflin, Eddie Brennan, J. J. Delaney, Tommy Walsh, T. J. Reid and Richie Hogan. He has constantly unearthed new hurling talent to keep Kilkenny at the top of the pile.

Cody's prowess on the sideline was emphasised in an unusual twist after the All-Ireland final of 2008. Kilkenny had romped to a 3-30 to 1-13 victory over Waterford to secure Cody's sixth title as manager. To honour the occasion, the RTÉ analysis panel took the surprising step of naming him Man of the Match. He was awarded the Freedom of Kilkenny City the same year.

As a player, Cody also enjoyed the taste of success at the highest level with Kilkenny. He played his club hurling with James Stephens before making the county senior panel in 1973, and he remained with the team until 1985. He made 24 championship appearances and won three All-Ireland titles, along with two national hurling leagues and four Leinster medals. He was team captain when Kilkenny won the Liam MacCarthy in 1982 and was awarded All-Stars in 1975 and 1982.

Other accolades Cody has collected throughout the years include the Philips Manager of the Year award in 2003, the Hotel Kilkenny and Kilkenny People Sports Star Supreme Award in 2009, and an honorary doctorate from UCC in 2012.

KILKENNY MANAGER
Brian Cody is lifted on the shoulders of Kilkenny supporters after his side's victory in the 2008 All-Ireland senior hurling final. Cody was chosen as RTÉ's Man of the Match after this game.

Hurling Managers: Ger Loughnane

Ger Loughnane's reign as the Clare senior hurling manager transformed the landscape of hurling.

He brought a new passion and intensity to training sessions as well as a mental toughness to his team, a combination that created a new era in Clare hurling and beyond.

GER LOUGHNANE.

Loughnane played his club hurling with Feakle and attended the famous St Flannan's College in Ennis before representing Clare at minor, under-21 and senior level. He made his senior debut for the Banner County in 1973 and continued to wear the Clare jersey until 1988. His own playing career was successful and he was awarded Clare's first ever All-Star in 1974. He went on to win two national hurling leagues in 1977 and 1978 and also played for Munster in the Railway Cup.

Loughnane first became involved with the management of the Clare senior hurlers in 1991 when he was appointed assistant to Len Gaynor. He was later dropped from the management team, but returned in 1993 before replacing Gaynor as senior manager in 1994, tasked with preparing Clare for the 1995 season. His career as senior manager got off to a good start when his side reached the national hurling league final and also beat Limerick in the 1995 Munster final. This was the first time the county had won a provincial title since 1932.

GER LOUGHNANE
with the Liam
MacCarthy Cup
in 1995.

MARTIN MCHUGH, MICHAEL LYSTER AND GER LOUGHNANE in the RTÉ studio.

The Munster trophy wasn't the last silverware Clare would win in 1995. After defeating a much-fancied Galway team in the All-Ireland semi-finals, they went on to beat reigning All-Ireland champions

Offaly in the All-Ireland final at Croke Park on 3 September 1995. Loughnane had succeeded in bringing the Liam MacCarthy to Clare for the first time in 81 years.

Loughnane remained at the helm of the Clare team and, after an early exit in 1996, the side were back in the All-Ireland final in 1997 where they faced neighbours Tipperary. As a result of the newly introduced 'back door system', this was the first all-Munster All-Ireland final ever played. Clare came from behind at half-time in a classic encounter to claim the All-Ireland senior title with a final scoreline of Clare 0-20, Tipperary 2-13.

The man from Feakle led Clare to another Munster title in 1998 before eventually parting company with the team in 2000. On his departure, he left behind a county transformed. Clare had achieved at the highest levels of hurling and a new belief in themselves remained.

In his later career, Loughnane spent time as manager of the Galway senior hurlers and is now a regular panellist on RTÉ's Gaelic games analysis programme, *The Sunday Game*.

GAA Teams of the Millennium

As the new millennium approached, the GAA announced that in partnership with An Post a football and hurling team of the millennium would be chosen, with the 15 positions on each team filled by the best player to have played in that position.

MEMBERS of the Football Team of the Millennium at the official launch in August 1999.

Both the hurling and football teams were selected by a panel of former GAA presidents and sports journalists, with An Post issuing commemorative stamps to mark the occasion.

In August 1999, the An Post/GAA Football Team of the Millennium was revealed, provoking much debate throughout the country. Of the six Kerry players named on the team, only two – Pat Spillane and Mikey Sheehy – were from the great Kerry team of the 1970s, while none of the Dublin players from that era were included. The football team in full was Danno Keeffe (Kerry), Enda Colleran (Galway), Joe Keohane (Kerry), Seán Flanagan (Mayo), Seán Murphy (Kerry), John Joe Reilly (Cavan), Martin O'Connell (Meath), Mick O'Connell (Kerry), Tommy Murphy (Laois), Seán O'Neill (Down), Seán Purcell (Galway), Pat Spillane (Kerry), Mikey Sheehy (Kerry), Tom Langan (Mayo) and Kevin Heffernan (Dublin). None of the then current players were included in the team, the most recent player being Martin O'Connell, who had won the All-Ireland with Meath in 1996.

In July 2000, the An Post/GAA Hurling Team of the Millennium was revealed. The team varied on only two positions from the 1984 Team of the Century – Brian Whelahan (Offaly) replaced Jimmy Finn (Tipperary) at right-back, while Ray Cummins (Cork) was awarded the full-forward berth in place of Nicky Rackard (Wexford). The hurling team in full was Tony Reddin (Tipperary), Bobby Rackard (Wexford), Nick O'Donnell (Wexford), John Doyle (Tipperary), Brian Whelahan (Offaly), John Keane (Waterford), Paddy Phelan (Kilkenny), Lory Meagher (Kilkenny), Jack Lynch (Cork), Christy Ring (Cork), Mick Mackey (Limerick), Jim Langton (Kilkenny), Jimmy Doyle (Tipperary), Ray Cummins (Cork) and Eddie Keher (Kilkenny). Whelahan was the solitary current player, with only six of the 15 men alive to see their names being included on the team. While Kilkenny had four players on the team, the omission of D. J. Carey, widely regarded as the greatest player of his generation, caused consternation, particularly in Kilkenny.

MEMBERS of the Hurling Team of the Millennium at the official launch in July 2000.

The All-Star Awards

The All-Stars are presented annually to the best player of the year in each field position in both hurling and Gaelic football.

Fifteen trophies are presented in each code. Since 2011, the awards have been presented jointly by the GAA and the GPA (Gaelic Players Association).

1971: The first All-Stars presentation banquet was held on 15 December.

1972: The traditional All-Star trip first took place, with the All-Star hurling and football teams going on tour to San Francisco.

1973: Limerick hurler Pat Hartigan claimed his second All-Star accolade following his side's victory over Kilkenny in the All-Ireland final. Hartigan went on to receive further All-Star awards in 1974 and 1975.

1974: Phil 'Fan' Larkin of Kilkenny picked up his second All-Star award. When his son Philip was named on the All-Star hurling team of 2002, the Larkins became the first father and son to receive All-Star honours in hurling.

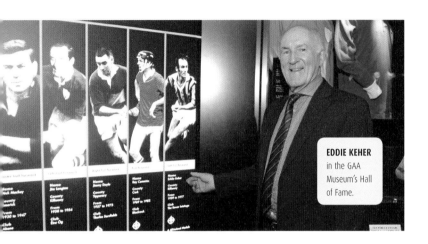

EDDIE KEHER
in the GAA
Museum's Hall
of Fame.

1975: Eddie Keher from the Inistioge club in Kilkenny was awarded the last of his five All-Stars for hurling.

1976: Kerry's Pat Spillane took the first of his impressive nine football All-Star awards.

1977: Joe Kernan of Armagh claimed his first All-Star Award at midfield.

1978: Ger Power from Kerry is one of an elite group of footballers who have been awarded All-Stars in both the backs and forwards. Having been honoured at left half-back in 1975 and 1976, Power went on to receive awards at right half-forward (1978, 1979 and 1980) and at left full-forward (1986).

1979: Dermot Earley Senior received his first All-Star award in 1974 and was honoured again in 1979 following an outstanding year with Roscommon. The Earley All-Star tradition continued in 1998 when Dermot Earley Junior was named on the All-Star football team representing Kildare. Eugene 'Nudie' Hughes became the first Monaghan footballer to be awarded an All-Star.

1980: Joe Connolly was named on the All-Star hurling team after he captained Galway to All-Ireland success.

1981: Kerry continued their presence on the All-Star football team when Páidí Ó Sé picked up the first of his five All-Star accolades.

1982: Offaly took seven All-Star awards in 1982 following their dramatic victory over Kerry in the All-Ireland senior football final.

1983: Nicky English was the only Tipperary player named on the All-Star hurling team of 1983. He won six All-Stars in total (1983, 1984, 1985, 1987, 1988 and 1989).

1984: The GAA's centenary year was celebrated in Cork when the county picked up six places on the 1984 All-Star hurling team. Dublin goalkeeper John O'Leary was also awarded the first of his five football All-Stars.

1985: Pat Critchley won Laois's first All-Star award when he was named at midfield on the All-Star hurling team.

1986: Corkman Jimmy Barry-Murphy won the last of his seven All-Star awards in 1986. One of the most successful dual players in Gaelic games history, he won two All-Stars for football and five for hurling.

1987: Galway half-back Pete Finnerty received his third hurling

All-Star accolade. He would go on to receive two more All-Stars, in 1988 and 1990.

1988: Antrim's Ciarán Barr became Ulster's first hurling All-Star when he was named at centre-forward on the All-Star hurling team.

1989: Tipperary brothers Conal and Cormac Bonnar were both named in the full-forward line of the All-Star hurling team. Their brother Colm had been honoured with an All-Star at midfield the previous year.

1990: Kevin O'Brien of Wicklow claimed the county's first and only All-Star award. The Baltinglass native was named at full-forward on the All-Star football team.

1991: D. J. Carey of Kilkenny won the first of his impressive nine hurling All-Star awards in 1991 and the last in 2002.

1992: Donegal were All-Ireland football champions in 1992 and secured seven All-Stars. Brothers Martin and James McHugh were among those selected.

CIARÁN BARR of Antrim.

KEVIN O'BRIEN, Wicklow's first All-Star.

1993: Derry won their first All-Ireland football championship title and received seven All-Star awards.

1994: A year of controversy as Hurler of the Year Brian Whelahan was omitted from the All-Star hurling team of 1994. Whelahan went on to be named at left-wing

back on the Hurling Team of the Millennium. In football, Tyrone's Peter Canavan was honoured with his first All-Star. Leitrim picked up their second All-Star when Seán Quinn won in the year that Leitrim won the Connacht football final.

1995: Clare's All-Ireland hurling success under Ger Loughnane earned them eight places on the 1995 All-Star team.

1996: Martin O'Connell of Meath picked up a fourth football All-Star in 1996. In the hurling, All-Ireland champions Wexford dominated with seven awards.

1997: Kildare gained three football All-Stars for the first time. In hurling, Clare's Brian Lohan received the third of his four awards.

SEAMUS QUINN.

1998: Tipperary gained their first football All-Star in 1998 when

ANTHONY TOHILL.

Declan Browne was selected in the full-forward line. Galway were honoured with seven football awards following their All-Ireland final victory.

1999: Meath were well-represented on the 1999 All-Star football team after a successful All-Ireland campaign. The county took home seven awards – their largest haul to date. Paddy Reynolds was chosen at left half-back, 28 years after his father Pat had been honoured in the same position. Graham Geraghty was named at full-forward, having received an award in the backline in 1994.

2000: Kilkenny claimed nine places on the All-Star hurling team.

2001: Westmeath joined the football All-Star ranks for the first time in 2001 when Rory O'Connell

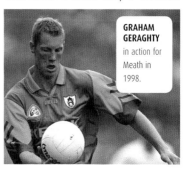

GRAHAM GERAGHTY in action for Meath in 1998.

from Athlone received the award at midfield. Roscommon's Francie Grehan received the county's first All-Star in 10 years.

2002: Armagh's All-Ireland victory was the GAA story of the year and Joe Kernan's team received six All-Stars. There were celebrations in Sligo when Eamonn O'Hara was honoured with the county's first award since 1974.

2003: Tyrone's first All-Ireland football success was reflected in the All-Star line-up and the county received seven awards.

2004: The 1,000th All-Star award was presented to Paul Galvin of Finuge, County Kerry.

2005: Tyrone dominated the All-Star football selection with eight players awarded following their All-Ireland winning campaign.

2006: Kilkenny's Tommy Walsh continued his All-Star streak, picking up his fourth hurling award. Incredibly, Walsh went on to win nine All-Stars in nine successive years. The unbroken streak ended in 2011 and by that time Walsh had been named in five different positions on nine All-Star hurling teams – a unique achievement.

SLIGO
All-Star
Eamonn O'Hara.

2007: The Waterford hurlers received five All-Stars, but All-Ireland champions Kilkenny dominated again, with a haul of six places on the All-Star hurling team. In football, it was a special night for Kerry's Ó Sé family. For the first time in the history of the All-Stars three brothers – Marc, Tomás and Darragh – were selected in the same year. Marc was also named Footballer of the Year.

TOMMY WALSH
with his All-Star Hurling Award in 2011.

2008: Westmeath men Gary Connaughton and John Keane both received football All-Stars. In hurling, Joe Canning of Galway received his first All-Star award and was also named Young Hurler of the Year.

2009: The Kerry footballers were represented in every positional line of the 2009 All-Star football team. Notably, Tadgh Kennelly received his award after becoming the first man to win both an All-Ireland football championship and an AFL premiership.

2010: Louth claimed their first All-Star when footballer Paddy Keenan represented the county at midfield.

2011: Dublin goalkeeper Stephen Cluxton received his fourth All-Star in 2011 after conceding just three goals and scoring 13 points. In the same year, Bernard Brogan succeeded his brother Alan as Footballer of the Year and both were named on the All-Star football team.

2012: 'King' Henry Shefflin of Kilkenny made history when he became the first player to win an 11th All-Star in either code.

2013: In recognition of their All-Ireland hurling success, Clare received eight All-Stars. Centre-forward Tony Kelly was named both Hurler of the Year and Young Hurler of the Year. On the football side, Kerry's Colm 'Gooch' Cooper picked up a seventh All-Star.

PADDY KEENAN in action for Louth against Kildare 2014.

2014: The All-Ireland football title was claimed by a young Kerry team who received five All-Star nods. In all there were six first-time football recipients this year, including Paul Murphy, James McCarthy, Peter Crowley, David Moran, Diarmuid Connolly and Cillian O'Connor.

2015: Dublin won the All-Ireland football title for the third time in five years, with seven of their players receiving an All-Star. Jack McCaffrey won an All-Star and the Footballer of the Year award – Jack was Young Footballer of the Year in 2013. T. J. Reid from Kilkenny won an All-Star and the Hurler of the Year award, rounding off an excellent year for T.J., who also captained his club Ballyhale Shamrocks to All-Ireland club glory on St Patrick's Day in Croke Park.

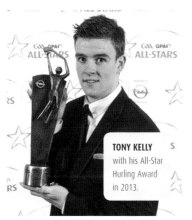

TONY KELLY with his All-Star Hurling Award in 2013.

The Dual Player

LIAM CURRAMS
in Croke Park
in 2010.

'Dual player' is a GAA term used to describe a player who plays both hurling and Gaelic football.

The demands of training in the modern era of Gaelic games mean there are fewer dual players than in previous years. A dual player has always been looked upon with respect in the GAA community due to the intricacies of honing the skills of both codes. Throughout the years, there have been many who have played both hurling and Gaelic football, but few have managed to play both sports at senior level for their county. Some famous inter-county dual players include former taoiseach of Ireland Jack Lynch (Cork), Liam Currams (Offaly), Teddy McCarthy (Cork), Paddy Mackey (Wexford) and Jimmy Barry-Murphy (Cork).

JACK LYNCH

As well as a successful political career which saw him hold the office of Taoiseach (prime minister) from 1977 to 1979, Jack Lynch was equally effective as both a hurler and Gaelic footballer and was known for his speed and strength. He is the only player to have won six All-Ireland medals in a row: for hurling in 1941, 1942, 1943, 1944 and 1946 and for football in 1945. On the football side, Lynch played at club level with St

Nicholas and won an All-Ireland title as well as two Munster championships with Cork. His hurling club was the famous Glen Rovers. Lynch won 11 county titles with the side. At inter-county level, he claimed five All-Ireland senior hurling titles with Cork and six Munster championship medals. Lynch played hurling for Cork from 1936 to 1950 and football from 1939 to 1949. Lynch's medals are now on display in the GAA Museum at Croke Park.

Family Ties

Through the playing of Gaelic games, the GAA has produced families with incredible records that have continued through generations.

THE Ó SÉ
brothers from Kerry.

There are fathers and sons, mothers and daughters and brothers and sisters who have achieved success at the highest level with both club and county. Some of the GAA's most famous families include the Rackards from Wexford, the Cannings of Portumna in Galway, the Kernans from Crossmaglen in Armagh, the Dooley brothers from Offaly, Donegal's McHugh family, the Brogans of Dublin and the Ó Sé family of Kerry.

Interestingly, the Larkin family from Kilkenny hold a unique record in hurling history, with All-Ireland medals won by grandfather, father and son, between 1932 and 2003. There is only one set of four brothers to have won All-Ireland senior hurling medals – Johnny, Paddy, Mick and Tommy Leahy of Boherlahan in Tipperary. The family record for the greatest number of All-Ireland senior hurling medals goes to the Doyles of Mooncoin, County Kilkenny – Eddie, Dick and Mick. Between them they won 19 All-Ireland senior hurling medals during Kilkenny's first golden era from 1904 to 1913, when the county claimed seven All-Irelands. For four of these – 1907, 1909, 1911 and 1912 – all three brothers featured in the starting team.

RELATIVES OF THE LEAHY BROTHERS at the launch of the GAA Dynasties exhibition in the GAA Museum, 2015.

The Donnellans of Galway are another family who have produced three generations of All-Ireland winners, this time in the Gaelic football code. Mick Donnellan from Dunmore won an All-Ireland senior medal in 1925, and his son John was part of the famous three-in-a-row Galway team of 1964–66. In 1998 and 2001 John's son Michael enjoyed All-Ireland success and completed a hat-trick of senior All-Ireland medals for the Donnellan family.

MICHAEL DONNELLAN
in action in 1998.

Did you know?

· Patrick O'Keeffe (1893) and John O'Keeffe (1919) from Cork were the first father and son to win All-Ireland medals in either hurling or football on the field of play.

· Kerry's John Joe Sheehy (1926 and 1930) and Seán Óg Sheehy (1962) are the only father and son to captain All-Ireland winning teams.

- Fathers and sons who have won All-Ireland medals with different counties include the Fergusons, Terry and Des. Terry won back-to-back titles with Meath in 1987 and 1988, while his dad Des won with Dublin in 1958 and 1963.

- Kilkenny's Angela Downey and her twin sister Ann have won every honour in camogie and between them have 24 All-Ireland senior medals. Their father, Shem Downey, also won an All-Ireland hurling medal with Kilkenny.

- In 2005, the Leinster senior football trophy was named in honour of Bill Delaney. Bill and his three brothers – Chris, Jack and Mick – from Laois won 18 Railway Cups between them from 1928 to 1946.

- In 1990 seven Fennelly brothers – Kevin, Michael, Seán, Ger, Dermot, Brendan and Liam – all won All-Ireland club hurling championship medals with Ballyhale Shamrocks of Kilkenny.

- Five Meehan brothers from Caltra in Galway won the All-Ireland club football championship in 2004. Enda, Declan, Tomás, Michael and Noel scored 12 points between them in the final.

CALTRA CAPTAIN NOEL MEEHAN

lifts the Tommy Moore Cup in 2004.

- The Spillanes of Templenoe in Kerry hold the record for the most All-Ireland senior football medals won by one family. From 1975 to 1987, brothers Pat, Tom and Mick won 19 All-Ireland senior championship medals. They are also the only three brothers to have won three All-Ireland senior medals in three consecutive years – from 1984 to 1986.

GPA and WGPA

The Gaelic Players Association was founded in 1999 by a group of former inter-county players.

The aim of the association is to support inter-county GAA players in terms of their health, personal development and education and career development.

In April 2010, the GPA was officially recognised by the GAA as the representative body for inter-county players. Former Dublin GAA player Dessie Farrell is the CEO of the GPA.

AOIFE LANE, chairperson of the WGPA, speaking in January 2015.

The Women's Gaelic Players Association (WGPA) was launched in January 2015. They have similar aspirations and goals as the GPA, representing female players in camogie and ladies football. They aspire to having official recognition for their Association in time.

MEMBERS of the GPA.

The Cancelled All-Irelands

In the history of the GAA, five All-Ireland finals have not taken place: the 1888 football and hurling finals, the 1910 football final, the 1911 hurling final and the 1925 football final.

The 1888 hurling and football championships were cancelled due to the American Invasion Tour. 1888 was the first time the competition was based on provincial championships, with four provincial competitions completed (Kilkenny won both

the Leinster hurling and football championship; Tipperary won the Munster football, while Monaghan won the Ulster title.) With the exodus of the best GAA hurlers, athletes and administrators to the US, the championships for 1888 were not completed.

The 1910 All-Ireland senior football final between Kerry and Louth (a keenly anticipated repeat of the 1909 All-Ireland final fixture) was fixed for Jones's Road, on 13 November 1910. The Kerry team arranged to travel to Dublin on Saturday, 12 November, on the 3.20 pm train from Tralee. However, when the Great Southern and Western Railway Company refused the Kerry team's requests to reserve a carriage for the team and to provide excursion-rate tickets for 20 fans who wanted to travel with them, the team took the decision not to contest the final. (The railway company later agreed to reserve a carriage but refused to supply the extra tickets for the fans.) The GAA Central Council subsequently awarded the championship to Louth.

RAILWAY
terminus in Killarney, Kerry, c.1890s.

The 1911 All-Ireland senior hurling final between Kilkenny and Limerick was scheduled for 18 February 1912 in the Cork Athletic Grounds. Up to 14,000 people travelled to Cork to watch this game, but it rained so heavily that day that the match was cancelled and rearranged for 12 May 1912 in Thurles. While Kilkenny were willing to play in Thurles, the Limerick team refused, and the final was never played. The Central Council did, however, organise a 'substitute final' between Kilkenny and Tipperary, which Kilkenny won.

The 1925 All-Ireland senior football final was not played due to a series of objections and counter-objections. While Kerry had beaten Cavan in the first semi-final, the two teams had fielded illegal players and both were disqualified from the competition. In the other semi-final, Mayo beat Wexford, so it looked like the title would be awarded to a Connacht team for the first time in the GAA's history. However, Mayo had been nominated to represent Connacht in the semi-final, as the Connacht championship was running way behind schedule, and when the Connacht final was eventually played, Galway defeated Mayo. The Central Council then controversially awarded the 1925 All-Ireland title to Galway, despite the fact that no final had actually been played.

ALL-IRELAND medal awarded in 1925 to Patrick Jennings of Galway, even though no final was played that year.

The 1895 Virtual All-Ireland

The All-Ireland senior football final of 1895 was one of the more curious incidents in GAA history.

MEDAL
awarded to the
1895 Meath team.

The final was actually played on 15 March 1896 between Tipperary and Meath. It was the first time Meath reached the final, and it was Tipperary's second appearance. This was also a significant game in the history of the GAA as it was the first All-Ireland final held at Jones's Road.

At this time counties were represented in the All-Ireland finals by the club that won the county championship. Meath were represented by Navan club Pierce O'Mahony and Tipperary were represented by Arravale Rovers. At the end of the match, Tipperary won by a point, the final score being 0-4 to 0-3.

However, after the match referee J. Kenny realised he had made an error in calculating the final score. The match had in fact been a draw.

He highlighted his error to the officials on the GAA Central Council.

Meath did not contest the result and Tipperary remained champions. In recognition of this, the GAA created the Virtual All-Ireland medals to present to the players on the Meath team. Jewellers Moore & Co. of Grafton Street made 9-ct rose-gold medals inscribed 'Virtual Championship of Ireland'.

PLAQUE unveiled in 1996 to mark the 1895 Virtual All-Ireland.

Unveiled by Seán Boothman, Uachtarán Cumann Lúthchleas Gael
15 Márta 1996
to commemorate the first All Ireland Finals played in Croke Park, 15 Márta 1896
Iomáint
Tubberadora V Tullaroan
Peil
Arravale Rovers V Pierce O'Mahonys
1896 — 1996

Four-in-a-Row

Occasionally a team emerges which dominates a competition for a number of years.

Five times in GAA history a county has won four All-Ireland senior titles in succession, but none have ever won five-in-a-row.

THE 1918 WEXFORD FOOTBALL TEAM, which completed Wexford's four-in-a-row.

1. From 1915 to 1918, Wexford's footballers defeated Kerry, Clare, Mayo and Tipperary to become the first team ever to win four-in-a-row.

2. Kerry's first football four-in-a-row came in 1932 with a team inspired by legendary players such as Dan O'Keeffe, John Joe Sheehy and Con Brosnan.

3. Cork dominated hurling from 1941 to 1944, defeating Dublin three times and Antrim once to become the first hurling side to win four consecutive All-Ireland senior hurling titles.

4. Kerry struck again in the late 1970s and early 1980s to win four All-Ireland senior football titles between 1978 and 1981.

5. Kilkenny's hurlers dominated the first decade of the new millennium, winning seven All-Ireland senior titles and becoming only the second county to win four all-Ireland senior hurling championships in a row between 2006 and 2009.

KERRY CAPTAIN GER POWER
lifts the Sam Maguire Cup in 1980.

KILKENNY'S BRIAN HOGAN
lifts the Liam MacCarthy Cup in 2009.

The Thunder and Lightning Final

On 3 September 1939, a crowd of 39,302 made their way to Croke Park in the rain to watch the All-Ireland senior hurling final between Kilkenny and Cork.

MATCH PROGRAMME

cover for the 1939 All-Ireland senior hurling final.

Due to the terrible weather conditions that this game was played in, it became known as the 'Thunder and Lightning Final'.

Coincidentally, at 11.00 that morning, Britain had declared war on Germany: before the day had ended, Britain, France, India, Australia and New Zealand were all at war with Germany.

While the first half of the game passed without major incident, with Kilkenny going into the interval with a lead of 2-04 to 1-01, approximately 10 minutes into the second half the rain started to fall heavily, with thunder and vivid flashes of forked lightning over the stadium. Uncovered spectators sought shelter elsewhere

MATCH TICKET for the 1939 All-Ireland senior hurling final.

in the stands, while the press corps, seated in the front seats of the Cusack Stand, were washed out and eventually had to vacate their positions. The Cork hurlers were playing against the weather for the second half and, while it looked like the game would have to be called off, *The Cork Examiner* later reported that 'all of the players were eager on reaching a decision, and under extraordinarily abnormal conditions the match was continued to a desperate finish.'

During the closing stages of the game, Cork scored a goal from a long-range free to level the match, but in a never-to-be-forgotten finish Jimmy Kelly scored the last-minute winning point for Kilkenny.

While all of the newspapers reported on the excitement of the game, the weather was one of the main talking points, with headlines such as 'Hurling Thrills End in Blinding Thunderstorm' and 'Thunderstorm Sweeps Ground At Crucial Point of Game'.

Séamus Darby's Goal in 1982

One of the most famous goals ever scored in an All-Ireland senior final was that by Offaly's Séamus Darby against Kerry in the closing stages of the 1982 football final at Croke Park.

The match saw Kerry and Offaly face each other in the final for the second year in a row, the Kerrymen having emerged victorious in 1981 to claim their fourth consecutive All-Ireland title. Huge hype then surrounded the Kerry team in the lead-up to the 1982 final as they hoped to win an historic five All-Irelands in a row. But the five-in-a-row was not to be for this legendary Kerry side, due to an Offaly goal in the closing stages of the game.

SEAMUS DARBY scores Offaly's last-minute goal in 1982, denying Kerry a famous five All-Ireland Football titles in a row.

Despite a missed penalty in the second half, Kerry led by two points with two minutes to go in what had been a hard-fought contest. In a crucial move, Offaly full-back Liam Connor ran out of defence to send a high ball towards substitute Seamus Darby from Rhode. Darby fielded the ball and turned towards goal before striking the ball high and into the top corner of Kerry goalkeeper Charlie Nelligan's net. The ball was over the line and Offaly had won their third All-Ireland senior football title by a single point, denying Kerry their five-in-a-row dreams along the way. The final score in this memorable game was Offaly 1-15, Kerry 0-17.

SEAMUS DARBY
and Charlie Nelligan
meet in 2015.

Interestingly, Séamus Darby had come on as a substitute at corner forward with just seven minutes left to play. In interviews since then, he has claimed that his goal was one of the only touches of the ball he had that day, but it was enough to write him into the GAA history books. In 2005 his strike came in third place in a poll to find the Top 20 GAA Moments of the television era.

1991 Dublin and Meath

Old rivals Dublin and Meath lit up the summer of 1991, contesting four matches in the first round of the Leinster football championship. These games have become part of GAA folklore.

When the first outing on 2 June was a draw, it went to a replay. And the next two games were also draws, resulting in three replays in total.

KEVIN FOLEY'S goal was voted the No.1 goal on RTE's countdown of greatest football goals of all time.

The games were hard-fought close encounters. Supporters found it very difficult to obtain tickets as the popularity of the games grew with every drawn match.

The third replay and final game in the saga was played on 6 July, the date the Leinster senior

football final should have taken place. With minutes to go, Dublin were in the lead and on course to win the four-game saga.

However, Meath began to claw back the deficit. A goal in the final minutes by half-back Kevin Foley levelled the game. Wing-forward David 'Jinxy' Beggy scored a point and Meath won. After the match, both teams were honoured at the Mansion House with a reception hosted by the Lord Mayor of Dublin.

After playing eight games to win the Leinster championship, Meath reached the All-Ireland senior football final. They were comprehensively beaten by Down and Sam Maguire headed over the border for the first time in 23 years. It was the beginning of the Ulster four-in-a-row, with Donegal, Derry and Down winning the next three All-Ireland football championships.

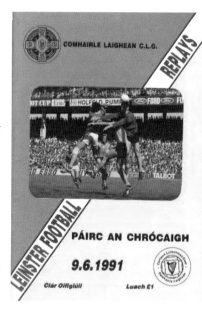

MATCH PROGRAMME cover for the first of the three replays.

Three GAA All-Ireland Senior Hurling Championship Final Replays in a Row: 2012, 2013 and 2014

The years 2012, 2013 and 2014 stand out in GAA history due to the fact that the All-Ireland senior hurling final in each of these years ended in a draw and forced a replay.

DAVID BURKE (GALWAY) AND JACKIE TYRELL (GALWAY) in action during the 2012 All-Ireland senior hurling final.

One All-Ireland senior hurling final ending with the sides level is unusual, but for three in a row to end with a tie was unprecedented. Until 2012, the All-Ireland senior hurling final had not ended in a draw since 1959. Interestingly, Liam O'Neill was GAA president for all three drawn finals.

2012: Kilkenny v Galway
Reigning All-Ireland champions Kilkenny faced Leinster champions

Galway in an epic battle at Croke Park on 9 September 2012. This was the fifth time the sides had faced each other in the final and they could not be separated at the final whistle, with the scoreboard reading Galway 2-13, Kilkenny 0-19.

The replay took place on 30 September. Galway named an unchanged side, while Kilkenny made two changes to their original line-out. The game was played once again in front of a full house at Croke Park. This time Kilkenny made no mistakes and emerged victorious on a 3-22 to 3-11 scoreline to break Galway hearts.

CLARE'S PAURIC COLLINS AND SHANE O'DONNELL celebrate after the 2013 All-Ireland senior hurling final.

2013: Clare v Cork

It was an all-Munster affair for the All-Ireland senior hurling final in 2013 when Cork faced Clare. This was the first time the two sides had ever met in the final. The game took place on 8

September and was a tense affair, with Cork leading by a single point with just one minute to go before the sliotar fell to Clare's right-back Domhnall O'Donovan, who levelled the game and forced the replay with his first ever championship point.

The replay took place on Saturday 28 September, with a later throw-in of 5.00 pm. It was the sixth time that Cork and Clare had faced off in 2013 and on this occasion the Banner County took the spoils.

An abundance of goals throughout a thrilling match resulted in a final score of Clare 5-16, Cork 3-16. Patrick Donnellan became the first Clareman since Anthony Daly in 1997 to lift the Liam MacCarthy.

2014: Kilkenny v Tipperary

After a year's absence, Kilkenny were back in the All-Ireland senior hurling final on 7 September, and this time they faced the might of Tipperary. The Cats had reached the final after defeating Limerick while Tipperary had beaten their old Munster rivals Cork in the semi-finals.

For the third year in a row, the teams could not be separated at the final whistle with the closing scoreline of Kilkenny 3-22, Tipperary 1-28. The replay was scheduled for 27 September and Kilkenny's experience in final replays saw them carve out a win by three points second time around. Notably, the result saw Kilkenny hero Henry Shefflin became the first player to win 10 All-Ireland senior hurling championship medals.

HENRY SHEFFLIN (KILKENNY) AND JAMES WOODLOCK (TIPPERARY) in action during the 2014 All-Ireland senior hurling final.

32 County Colours

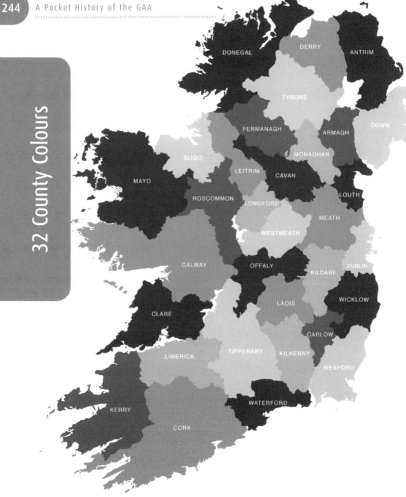

Connacht

SLIGO/SLIGEACH

MAYO/MAIGH EO

GALWAY/GAILLIMH

LONDON/LONDAIN

LEITRIM/LIATROIM

NEW YORK/NUA EABHRAC

New York and London compete in the Connacht championship.

ROSCOMMON/ROS COMÁIN

Leinster

CARLOW/
CEATHARLACH

DUBLIN/
ÁTH CLIATH

KILDARE/CILL
DARA

KILKENNY/CILL
CHAINNIGH

LAOIS/
LAOIS

LONGFORD/AN
LONGFORT

LOUTH/
AN LÚ

MEATH/
AN MHÍ

OFFALY/
UÍBH FHAILÍ

**WESTMEATH/
AN IARMHÍ**

**WEXFORD/
LOCH GARMAN**

**WICKLOW/CILL
MHANTÁIN**

Munster

CLARE/
AN CLÁR

CORK/
CORCAIGH

KERRY/
CIARRAÍ

LIMERICK/
LUIMNEACH

TIPPERARY/
TIOBRAID ÁRANN

WATERFORD/
PORT LÁIRGE

Ulster

ANTRIM/
AONTROIM

ARMAGH/
ARD MHACHA

CAVAN/
AN CABHÁN

DERRY/
DOIRE

DONEGAL/
DÚN NA NGALL

DOWN/AN DÚN

FERMANAGH/
FEAR MANACH

MONAGHAN/
MUINEACHÁN

TYRONE/
TÍR EOGHAIN

Presidents of the GAA

Maurice Davin, 1884–87
Edward Bennett, 1887
Maurice Davin, 1887–89
Peter Kelly, 1889–95
Frank Dineen, 1895–98
Michael Deering, 1898–1901
James Nowlan, 1901–21
Daniel McCarthy, 1921–24
Patrick Breen, 1924–26
Liam Clifford, 1926–28
Seán Ryan, 1928–32
Seán McCarthy, 1932–35
Robert O'Keeffe, 1935–38
Padraig McNamee, 1938–43
Seamus Gardiner, 1943–46
Daniel O Rourke, 1946–49
Michael Kehoe, 1949–52
M. V. O'Donoghue, 1952–55
Seamus McFerran, 1955–58
Dr J. J. Stuart, 1958–61
Aodh O'Broin, 1961–63
Alf Murray, 1964–67
Seamus Ó Riain, 1967–70
Pat Fanning, 1970–73
Dr Donal Keenan, 1973–76
Con Murphy, 1976–79
Paddy McFlynn, 1979–82
Paddy Buggy, 1982–84
Dr Mick Loftus, 1985–87
John Dowling, 1988–91

Peter Quinn, 1991–94
Jack Boothman, 1994–97
Joe McDonagh, 1997–2000
Seán McCague, 2000 –3
Seán Kelly, 2003–6
Nickey Brennan, 2006–9
Criostóir Ó Cuana, 2009–12
Liam O'Neill, 2012–15
Aogán Ó Fearghail, 2015–

General Secretaries/ Director Generals

Michael Cusack, 1884–85
John Wyse Power, 1884–87
John McKay, 1884–85
Timothy O'Riordan, 1885–89
John O'Reilly, 1885–87
James Moore, 1887–88
William Prendergast, 1888–89
P. R. Cleary, 1889–90
Maurice Moynihan, 1890–92
Patrick Tobin, 1891–94
David Walsh, 1894–95
Richard Blake, 1895–98
Frank B. Dineen, 1898–1901
Luke O'Toole, 1901–29
Padraig O'Caoimh, 1929– 64
Seán Ó Síocháin, 1964–79
Liam Mulvihill, 1979–2007
Páraic Duffy, 2008–

Did You Know?

- The most one-sided competitive match on record was between Wexford and Kildare in the Croke Cup hurling competition in 1897. Wexford won by 14-15 to 1-1.

- The most one-sided championship match was Offaly's win over Louth by 10-23 to nil in the 1910 Leinster senior hurling championship.

- Kilkenny had the shortest reign as All-Ireland senior hurling champions. On 30 June 1907, they beat Cork 7-7 to 2-9 in the 1905 final. Two weeks later they were defeated by Dublin in the 1906 Leinster hurling final.

- The only scoreless draw in GAA history occurred in the 1895 Munster football championship between Cork and Kerry in Limerick. With five minutes to go the teams were scoreless when the ball burst and a replacement could not be found. The referee declared the match a draw.

- In 1906 the Kerry footballers drew with Mayo on the scoreline of 0-1 to 0-1.

- In 1924 Naas drew with Caragh in a seven-a-side football match organised in connection with a local carnival. The medals sat in the carnival secretary's drawer until he noticed that the match had not been replayed. The replay took place in 1959, 35 years after the original game. The teams were made up of the sons of the original players.

- When Kilkenny met Wexford in the 1890 Leinster football championship in Waterford, the referee discovered that he had no football. Someone was dispatched to town to buy another but by the time the game was finished many Wexford supporters had missed the steamer back to New Ross.

- Meath were once Leinster football champions for 20 minutes. At 1.45 pm on 22 October 1911 they were awarded the title because their opponents Kilkenny had failed to show. At 2.15 pm Kilkenny turned up, the title was taken from Meath and the match was played, Kilkenny eventually winning a replay by 2-4 to 1-1.